SAY NO TO
CANCER

D1428782

Other books by Patrick Holford

SAY NO TO

CANCER

PATRICK HOLFORD

PIATKUS

✿ *Visit the Piatkus website!*

Piatkus publishes a wide range of bestselling fiction and non-fiction, including books on health, mind, body & spirit, sex, self-help, cookery, biography and the paranormal.

If you want to:
- read descriptions of our popular titles
- buy our books over the internet
- take advantage of our special offers
- enter our monthly competition
- learn more about your favourite Piatkus authors

VISIT OUR WEBSITE AT: www.piatkus.co.uk

© 1999 by Patrick Holford

First published in 1999 by
Piatkus Books Ltd
5 Windmill Street, London W1T 2JA
email: info@piatkus.co.uk

Reprinted 2001, 2002, 2003, 2004, 2005

The moral rights of the author has been asserted

A catalogue record for this book is available from the British Library

ISBN 0 7499 1953 1

Designed by Paul Saunders

Typeset by Phoenix Photosetting, Chatham, Kent
Printed and bound in Great Britain by
Mackays of Chatham Ltd, Chatham, Kent

CONTENTS

PART 3:   ANTI-CANCER LIFESTYLE FACTORS

PART 4:   ANTI-CANCER NUTRIENTS

PART 5:   HOW TO AVOID CANCER

PART 6:   A – Z OF NUTRITIONAL HEALING   163

Cancers: Breast ● Cervical ● Colorectal
● Endometrial ● Kidney and Bladder ● Liver
● Lung ● Mouth, Throat and Oesophagus ● Ovarian
● Pancreas ● Prostate ● Skin ● Stomach ● Testicular

ACKNOWLEDGEMENTS

Cancer is a complex subject and I am indebted to all the researchers whose work is helping to find a way forward. I am most indebted to nutrition and cancer expert Dr Richard Passwater – for his excellent review of cancer studies, for checking the manuscript and for his continued guidance as this story unfolds. My thanks also go to the team at the World Cancer Research Fund whose excellent 670-page document has helped put diet top of the anti-cancer agenda. Finally, very special thank-you to Natalie Savona for her researching, editing and invaluable assistance, and to Kelly Davis and Rachel Winning at Piatkus for their editorial advice, support and encouragement.

GUIDE TO ABBREVIATIONS AND MEASURES

1 gram (g) = 1000 milligrams (mg) = 1 000 000 micrograms (mcg or μg). Most vitamins are measured in milligrams or micrograms. Vitamins A, D and E are also measured in International Units (iu), a measurement designed to standardise the different forms of these vitamins which have different potencies.

1mcg of retinol (mcgRE) = 3.3iu of vitamin A (RE = Retinol Equivalents)
1mcgRE of beta-carotene = 6mcg of beta-carotene
100iu of vitamin D = 2.5mcg
100iu of vitamin E = 67mg
1 pound (lb) = 16 ounces (oz) 2.2lb = 1 kilogram (kg)
In this book calories means kilocalories (kcal)

REFERENCES AND FURTHER SOURCES OF INFORMATION

Hundreds of references from respected scientific literature have been used in writing this book. References for those specific studies referred to, are listed on page 175, together with further reading suggestions. Other supporting research for statements made is available from the Lamberts Library at the Institute for Optimum Nutrition (ION) (see page 190). Members are free to visit and study there. ION also has information services, including literature search and library search facilities, for those readers who want to access the scientific literature on specific subjects. On page 189 you will also find a Recommended Reading list which suggests the best books to read if you wish to dig deeper into the topics covered in each chapter.

INTRODUCTION

No diagnosis strikes more fear into the hearts of patients than that of cancer. Perceived as incurable, its cause unknown, cancer is today what the plague must have been in the eighteenth century. We live in fear of it and avoid talking about it. Meanwhile, as we hide our heads in the sand, cancer has grown to be the second most common cause of premature death in the Western world and is predicted to become the number one cause of death within 20 years. It is already the primary killer of people under the age of 50.

CANCER IS A 20TH-CENTURY INVENTION

Yet it may surprise you to know that cancer is, for the most part, a 20th-century invention. The top five cancers – lung, breast, stomach, colorectal and prostate – were more or less unheard of before the early 20th century. The growth in the incidence of cancer parallels the industrialisation and chemicalisation of our world. The more developed a country, the more cancer. The higher the per capita income, the higher the incidence of cancer.[1]

This is because most cancers are primarily the result of changes we have made to our total chemical environment – what we eat, drink and breathe. Changing patterns of cancer in the economically developed world show that cancer rates are strongly influenced by environmental factors. According to one of Britain's top medical scientists, Sir Richard Doll, 90 per cent of all cancers are caused by such environmental factors. The most conservative cancer experts say that at least 75 per cent of cancers are associated with environmental and lifestyle factors.

In the space of two generations, mankind has invented ten million new chemicals and unwittingly released thousands of them into the environment. Many are known to be carcinogens (i.e. they are capable of causing cancer). And we take these in (ingest them) in our food, air and water. Many are easily avoidable – but some are not.

We have, it seems, been digging our own graves with our knives and forks. Today's diet of refined foods, laced with chemicals and devoid of nutrients, is now thought to be the greatest single contributor to cancer risk. Conversely, by eating the right diet you can cut your risk of cancer by up to 40 per cent, says the World Cancer Research Fund. The European Commission estimates that a quarter of a million lives could be saved each year across the 12 member states through dietary changes alone. According to the Cancer Research Campaign, 'At least three out of four of all cancers are potentially preventable, but will only be avoided if the messages get through at a young age.'

But cancer isn't only about diet. We unknowingly expose ourselves to many cancer-causing chemicals in our homes and workplaces; minimising this exposure can also greatly reduce our risk of cancer.

BOOSTING YOUR IMMUNE SYSTEM

Avoiding or reducing known cancer-causing chemicals is just one side of the cancer equation. The other side is strengthening your own defences. Carcinogens are nothing new. They exist in nature, even in everyday health-promoting foods, but they don't necessarily present a problem because the body is designed to detoxify carcinogens. It's when your body's defences are weak, and you are exposed to too many carcinogens, that the trouble starts.

So boosting your immune system is clearly vital. Your risk of developing cancer really could be virtually eliminated by putting all this together: avoiding known carcinogens; eating the right diet; and boosting your immune system. The evidence presented in this book strongly suggests that you genuinely can 'say no to cancer'.

ARE WE WINNING THE CANCER WAR?

Despite the fact that we already know how to drastically reduce cancer risk, the sad truth is that we are not taking the necessary action – with a few notable exceptions. The incidence of lung cancer, for example, is now decreasing in the UK as fewer and fewer people smoke. Cervical cancer and cancer of the stomach are also on the decline. Despite this, the overall rate of cancer, which now strikes one in three and kills one in four, is still very much on the increase.

According to a UK survey by the East Anglian Cancer Intelligence Unit at Cambridge University, we are heading for a cancer epidemic.[2] While cancer is currently the second most common cause of death, within 20 years the risk of developing cancer at some time during your life will be greater than 50 per cent. The US National Cancer Institute also predicts an increase in death from cancer.

It is true that the incidence of some cancers is decreasing, but what is particularly worrying is the rise in hormone-related cancers. These are cancers of hormonally sensitive tissue which, in men, are cancer of the prostate and testes, and, in women, cancer of the breast, cervix, ovaries and womb (endometrium).

Take breast cancer, for example. Currently, one in 12 women develops breast cancer in the USA – one in eight in the UK. The incidence of a type of cervical cancer, adeno-carcinoma, has also gone up fourfold in 20 years. Within 20 years, one in four men is predicted to develop prostate cancer.[3] In truth, these cancers are occurring more frequently and earlier in people's lives than they were a decade ago. It is highly likely that dietary changes and our exposure to environmental toxins play a significant role in this.

In 1992, a statement signed by 69 highly respected medical and scientific experts in the USA stated, 'Over the last decade, some five million Americans died of cancer and there is growing evidence that a substantial proportion of these deaths was avoidable.'[4]

ARE WE EVEN FIGHTING IT?

The reason for their statement was to protest against the failure of the policies of government and cancer institutions. The same is true in the UK. Remarkably little research money is being spent on prevention, with most being directed towards variations on conventional treatment using surgery, drugs or chemotherapy.

Unfortunately conventional treatment, which is all rather medieval in concept (essentially to cut it out, burn it out or drug it out), has proven remarkably unsuccessful. Those in favour of current treatments argue that, for example in the case of breast cancer, the survival rate has increased from 60 to 75 per cent over the last 30 years. This represents a 15 per cent improvement, they claim. Yet the death rate from cancer over the same period has stayed the same. All that's happened is that people are being diagnosed earlier, and hence appear to survive longer.

While prevention is better than cure, the fact is that cancer prevention is not profitable. Most of the main cancer charities have very close links with the pharmaceutical and chemical industries. Some people believe that the main interest is in profiting from cancer treatment, rather than highlighting the true causes of cancer – namely the modern diet and over-exposure to cancer-causing chemicals. There is, however, a list of known factors associated with increasing cancer risk that they could try to avoid; and such advice can be obtained from a GP or a nutritionist.

PREVENTION IS BETTER THAN CURE

Prevention is as important for someone who doesn't have cancer as for someone who does. The easiest way to stay free of cancer is do all the right things in the first place, while people with an early diagnosis of cancer can often prevent its development or recurrence. Primary cancers are very rarely life-threatening. It is the secondaries, the cancers that follow, that claim all too many victims.

So, once diagnosed, it is absolutely essential to follow the right kind of diet, avoid carcinogens and boost your immune system. The purpose of this book is to explain what that means in practice. But first, it's worth knowing what causes cancer and how you can intervene to keep your body healthy.

HOW TO USE THIS BOOK

Cancer is a very complicated issue so I have structured this book to make it easy for you to understand what you need to do to reduce the risk.

Part 1 explains what cancer is, which factors influence its development, and why you can expect almost complete protection by following the advice in this book.

Part 2 reveals the connections between different foods and the development or avoidance of cancer. Reading this section will help you understand the basis for the practical recommendations later in the book.

Part 3 identifies the lifestyle and environmental risk factors for cancer – with particular recommendations in Chapter 17.

Part 4 gathers the evidence on how nutrients and other natural remedies can help you avoid cancer.

Part 5 offers clear, practical guidelines for staying free from cancer and, if you are a cancer patient, tells you how to maximise your recovery.

Finally, Part 6 gives you specific advice on risk factors, prevention and nutritional support for each kind of cancer.

MEDICAL ADVICE

Many of the strategies recommended here have proven to be very effective, but the recommendations in this book do not replace those of your doctor. If you wish to change your medication please consult your doctor.

PART 1

....

WHAT CAUSES
CANCER?

CHAPTER 1

WHAT IS CANCER?

It may surprise you to know that we all have cancer. Cancer occurs when cells start to behave differently from normal – growing, multiplying and spreading. It is like a revolution within the body, when a group of cells stops working in harmony with the whole organism and starts running riot. We all produce cancer cells, so the odd revolutionary cell is a very common occurrence. The immune system of a healthy person simply isolates and destroys such offenders before they develop to form a cancer mass, or tumour. However, in cancer, the immune system is overcome and the cancer spreads. Understanding how and why this happens is the key to preventing cancer.

An embryo turns into a baby, and eventually into a fully grown human, because our cells are programmed to multiply – two, four, eight, 16 and so on – until you have the 30 trillion or so cells that make up an adult. The early cells all look similar and then, as they develop, they start to look different from one another and take on specific roles in our bodies. Although most cells continue to be replaced throughout our lives, they generally stop growing or multiplying and basically settle down (like good citizens) to get on with their specific duties, respecting their neighbours.

If, however, a cell is damaged in some way it can start to behave more primitively, growing and multiplying, not respecting its neighbours, nor carrying out its specific function. This is a cancer cell. Most cancer cells will be detected by the immune system and weeded out. Some, however, appear more resistant, or can flourish because the immune system is weak.

They may then go on to develop clusters of such 'undifferentiated' cells. If the cells are not actually multiplying and do not pose an immediate risk, the growth is called a benign tumour. If, however, the cells are multiplying it is called a malignant tumour.

In due course the multiplying cancer cells become a cancer mass. Like any other cells, they need food to keep working and so the mass develops its own blood supply to provide this. Depending on where and how big the cancer mass is, symptoms may become apparent. During an autopsy after a different cause of death, many people are found to have a cancer mass without ever having been aware of it. These 'primary' cancers have different names, depending on the kind of tissue they occur in and their location. Most human cancers are carcinomas (carc = cancer; oma = tumour), malignant tumours that arise from epithelial cells. Melanomas (melano = black), for example, are cancerous growths of melanocytes, skin cells that produce the pigment melanin. Sarcoma is a general term for any cancer arising from muscle cells or connective tissues. For example, osteogenic sarcomas (osteo = bone; genic = origin), the most frequent type of childhood cancer, destroys bone tissue (connective tissue) and eventually spreads to other areas of the body. Leukaemia is a cancer of blood forming organs characterised by rapid growth and distorted development of leukocytes (white blood cells) and their precursors. Lymphoma is a malignant disease of lymphatic tissue, for example, lymph nodes. An example is Hodgkin's disease.

'Primary' cancer is rarely likely to be fatal. However, at some point, a more mobile 'metastatic' cancer cell may develop. These metastatic cells can leave the original cancer mass and

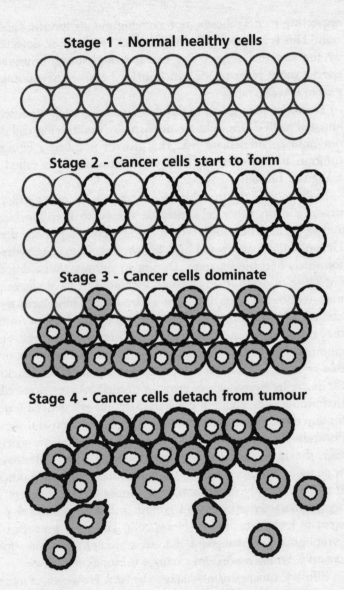

Stage 1 - Normal healthy cells

Stage 2 - Cancer cells start to form

Stage 3 - Cancer cells dominate

Stage 4 - Cancer cells detach from tumour

Figure 1 – Normal cells versus cancer cells

spread around the body, through the bloodstream or the lymphatic vessels. They can then lodge in different parts of the body and start multiplying there, resulting in what are known as 'secondary tumours'.

These secondaries are more insidious, much harder to treat and tend to spread and grow more quickly. Consequently, the average chance of surviving, once secondaries appear, is much lower.

WHAT'S THE AIM OF CONVENTIONAL TREATMENT?

The main focus of conventional cancer treatment is the early detection and then annihilation of the tumours. The earlier a cancer is detected, the better the chances of eliminating the primary tumour before it metastasizes (or spreads) and produces secondaries.

Early detection, however, is not without its problems. Mammograms, used to detect breast tumours, are capable of detecting microcalcifications (small calcium deposits) in the breasts which could never be felt before. These microcalcifications may not be cancer as we know it – whether or not they warrant treatment is a matter of debate. Mammograms also expose a woman to radiation, thereby increasing cancer risk. Some scientists therefore believe that routine mammography under the age of 50 for symptom-free women is unwarranted. The usual treatment for breast cancer is Tamoxifen, yet people who take it do just as well as those who don't.

There are three ways to annihilate a tumour – with surgery, radiation or chemotherapy. Some forms of cancer don't lend themselves to surgery (e.g. liver, brain, bone and blood), in which case chemotherapy – using drugs that are toxic to cancer cells – is employed. While these treatments can and do save lives, the trouble is they do so at a cost: each treatment is traumatic and damages the body. Recent advances in such therapies have attempted to minimise the damage – for example, to develop chemotherapeutic drugs that target only cancer cells and don't damage healthy cells.

Nutritional support is vital during these treatments – it can reduce side effects and speed up recovery (see Chapter 26). Yet conventional cancer therapies place remarkably little emphasis on eliminating the factors that cause cancer in the first place, or on boosting the body's natural defences to fight back and restore healthy cells.

WHAT INITIATES CANCER?

Cancer is the uncontrolled growth of cells. The key question is why do cells suddenly start growing and multiplying? There are many different kinds of cancers and no doubt many different answers to this question. However, in many cases, a major contributing factor is damage to the cell.

The outer membrane (or 'skin') of each cell contains sensors that tell it when to grow or multiply. If these sensors are damaged by an undesirable chemical, cancer can result. Each cell also contains instructions for its behaviour, and for the behaviour of future cells. These are contained within the genes which are written on the DNA, (the genetic blueprint material found in every single cell). If a chemical enters the body and damages the DNA, the cell can start to 'misbehave', dividing and producing more errant cells.

Some of us also have dormant genes that, if awakened by a particular stimulus, can trigger cancer. These cancer-causing genes are called oncogenes and can be activated by a number of undesirable chemicals. Factors that can trigger cancer are called carcinogens and they are fully discussed in Parts 2 and 3.

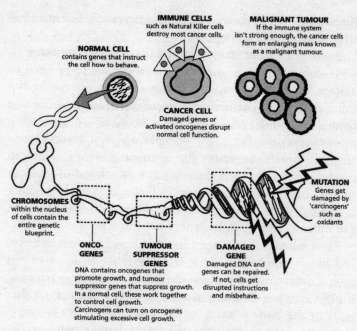

Figure 2 – The initiation of cancer

WHAT PROMOTES CANCER?

While this whole process of undesirable chemicals altering cell function marks the beginning of the cancer process, this alone is not enough for a person to develop a malignant tumour. Indeed, such cellular changes are happening within us all the time, producing individual pre-cancerous cells which are found and destroyed by our immune system.

In order for the cancer cells to survive and take over, they must multiply and invade surrounding tissue. The mass must then develop its own defences and blood supply. A number of substances and circumstances can help or hinder the cancer's progression to this stage. Some chemicals, for example, do not initiate cancer but do encourage its progression. Scientists call these epigenetic carcinogens.

Even if a cancer mass is promoted through exposure to undesirable chemicals, the cancer mass still has to progress to a stage where it is strong enough to fight off the body's immune system. The immune system makes large numbers of natural killer (NK) cells which are quite capable of destroying most cancer cells. But if, for example, a person drinks a lot of alcohol, which suppresses the immune system's ability to produce NK cells, then there is more likelihood of a cancer progressing. The combination of smoking and drinking is particularly inadvisable: the carcinogens in tobacco smoke can initiate cancer, while alcohol promotes it.

Even when a cancer mass has developed its own defences and blood supply, this alone is rarely fatal. Whether or not such a cancer mass goes into the metastatic phase – releasing mobile cancer cells that produce secondary cancers in other parts of the body – again depends on a person's chemistry. Some nutrients reduce the risk of metastasis, while other chemicals promote it.

In this book you will learn which nutrients and foods can protect you against cancer, at every stage, and also which chemicals you need to avoid.

CHAPTER 2

....

THE OXIDANT CONNECTION

A big part of the cancer equation, and one reason for the rapid development of cancer in the 20th century, is our increased exposure to cancer-causing factors, especially those that directly damage our genes. These include:

- Tobacco smoke
- Exhaust fumes
- Industrial pollution
- Burnt, browned or fried food
- Excessive sun exposure
- Radiation
- Viruses and bacteria

These and many other factors produce chemicals called oxidants (also known as 'free radicals' or 'free oxidising radicals'). Oxidants are a bit like the toxic exhaust of any burning process that involves oxygen. We even make oxidants in our bodies, when we 'burn' the carbohydrate we eat (to form energy) by reacting it with the oxygen we breathe in.

So, if you want to increase your risk of developing cancer, just stand in the main street of a polluted city, on a hot sunny day, when you have a cold, burning your skin, breathing in exhaust fumes, eating French fries and smoking a cigarette. Not many people do all these things at once, but many people's lifestyles do involve significant exposure to oxidants.

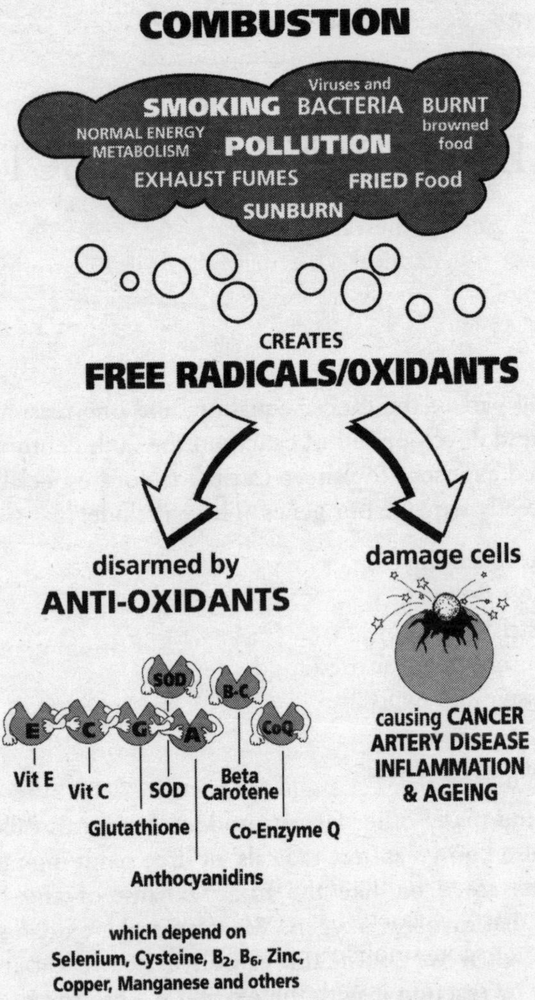

COMBUSTION

Viruses and
SMOKING BACTERIA   BURNT
browned
NORMAL ENERGY   food
METABOLISM **POLLUTION**

EXHAUST FUMES   **FRIED** Food

SUNBURN

CREATES
FREE RADICALS/OXIDANTS

disarmed by   damage cells
ANTI-OXIDANTS

causing **CANCER
ARTERY DISEASE
INFLAMMATION
& AGEING**

SOD   B-C

CoQ

E   C   G   A

Vit E   Vit C   SOD   Beta
Carotene

Glutathione   Co-Enzyme Q

Anthocyanidins

which depend on
**Selenium, Cysteine, B₂, B₆, Zinc,
Copper, Manganese and others**

Figure 3 – Oxidants and anti-oxidants

(The effects of smoking, radiation and sun exposure are discussed later, in Part 3.)

Conversely, if you very rarely eat burnt, browned or fried
food, spend little time in traffic, live in an unpolluted

environment, don't smoke, rarely get infections, and avoid exposure to strong sunlight then your cancer risk will be lower.

ANTI-OXIDANT PROTECTION

That's one side of the oxidant equation. The other side is anti-oxidants – chemicals that neutralise these harmful oxidants. There are literally hundreds of anti-oxidants, the best known of which are vitamins A, C and E. The evidence for the protective effect of taking in optimal amounts of these anti-cancer nutrients (discussed fully in Parts 2 and 4) is overwhelming.

The power of anti-oxidants is clearly illustrated by one survey published in *The Lancet* medical journal, which looked at the relationship between beta-carotene (the vegetable form of vitamin A) status and smoking.[5] They found that heavy smokers with a low beta-carotene status had a 6.5 per cent chance of developing lung cancer. On the other hand a heavy smoker with a high beta-carotene status only had a 0.8 per cent risk. So too did a non-smoker with a low beta-carotene status. Finally, those who had a high beta-carotene status and didn't smoke had no risk. This study shows that increasing your intake of anti-cancer nutrients is just as important as limiting your intake of carcinogens.

While the overall incidence of lung cancer is falling in countries where cigarette smoking is on the decline, lung cancer among non-smokers is actually rising.[6] This is almost certainly because of increasing levels of air pollution, particularly from diesel fuel, says Professor Simon Wolff, a toxicologist, who points out that 'in rural China, where people tend to smoke very heavily and where air pollution is much less, the difference in lung cancer rates between smokers and non-smokers is very small, and lung cancer rates are about one-tenth of the lung cancer rates in industrialised countries.'[7]

It is also likely that the diet in rural China is higher in anti-oxidants than the typical diet in industrialised countries. So there are two sides to the equation.

OXIDANT DAMAGE

We need to understand how oxidants do their damage in order to defend ourselves against cancer. Oxidants are unstable and dangerous because they have an uneven electrical charge (whereas a stable chemical has an even electrical charge). Oxidants are rather like amorous bachelors looking for partners. To complete themselves, they steal electrons from cells, homing in on either the membrane of the cell or the DNA because this is where the most 'double bonds' (atoms that are connected with two links) are found. These double bonds are particularly susceptible to oxidant damage.

Another source of double bonds is fat. The more unsaturated a fat, the more double bonds it contains. Polyunsaturated fats, such as sunflower oil, have plenty of double-bonds, and if you use it for frying – which generates very high temperatures – these double bonds can get damaged. Eating fried foods therefore increases your intake of oxidants, which, in turn, can start to damage your cells.

Anti-oxidants are real heroes. They mop up the dangerous oxidant 'sparks', but in the process, become oxidised and destablise themselves. If, however, they then meet another oxidant they can be 'reloaded'. Like a team of bomb disposal experts, anti-oxidants work together to defuse the dangerous chemical sparks called oxidants.

This synergistic partnership of anti-oxidants is very important. Key partnerships exist between different anti-oxidants which become inactivated once they've disarmed an oxidant. For example:

• Vitamin E is recycled by vitamin C and co-enzyme Q

- Vitamin C is recycled by glutathione and carotenoids (in carrots)
- Glutathione is recycled by anthocyanidins (in berries)

The sum of the whole is far greater than the sum of the parts. So, having a high intake of both vitamin C and E, or glutathione and anthocyanidins, can be much more protective than having a high level of just one of these nutrients on its own. The body can only completely detoxify many harmful substances if all these nutrients are present in the right amounts.

The synergy of nutrients is also vital because there are many different kinds of oxidants, each disarmed most effectively by a different kind of anti-oxidant. So, for all-round protection against all the oxidants that come your way, you need to take in a whole collection of anti-oxidants, including:

vitamin A
vitamin C
vitamin E
selenium
glutathione
anthocyanidins
carotenoids
co-enzyme Q

These nutrients are found in food and can also be taken as nutritional supplements but unfortunately this is only part of the story. There are many cancer-causing chemicals that don't cause oxidation, so just avoiding oxidants and increasing your intake of anti-oxidants can only offer partial protection. The next chapter looks at another factor – hormone-disrupting chemicals in our environment.

CHAPTER 3

·····································

HORMONES IN HAVOC

Evidence is accumulating that the high incidence of cancer of the breast, cervix and ovaries in women, and of the prostate and testes in men, is related to disturbed regulation of our hormones. All of these body tissues are especially sensitive to the effects of hormones. The rapid increase in breast cancer and prostate cancer (predicted to affect a quarter of all men by the year 2018) has raised concerns about a number of chemicals in our foods, homes and medicines that may be adding to our risk of developing cancer.

The probability of a person contracting these hormone-related cancers during their lifetime is shown below (comparing actual figures in 1985 to predicted figures in the years 2000 and 2015).

Hormone-related cancer incidence and risk

	1985	2000	2015	Increase in risk from 1985 to 2015
Breast (women)	8.6%	10.6%	13.1%	52%
Cervical (women)	1.5%	1.4%	1.6%	7%
Uterine (women)	1.2%	1.8%	2.2%	83%
Prostate (men)	7.1%	13.5%	23.7%	234%
Testicular (men)	0.4%	0.4%	0.6%	50%

Breast cancer incidence, for example, has nearly tripled in the last 30 years. It now affects one in eight women in Britain at some time in their life (compared to one in 22 in the 1940s) and rates are predicted to double again in the next 20 years. Meanwhile, rates of prostate cancer have doubled in the last 20 years and this disease now affects around one in ten men at some point in their life. By 2015 it is predicted to affect one in four.[8]

The current approaches to breast cancer are not having much effect on this worrying trend. While we are told that the five year survival rate, once a woman has been diagnosed with breast cancer, has improved (mainly due to earlier detection), the ultimate survival rate hasn't. What's more, breast cancer is occurring more frequently and earlier in women's lives than it was a decade ago.

HORMONE-DISRUPTING CHEMICALS

The fundamental question is, why are such cancers increasing and what can be done to reverse this? In one of the most extraordinary detective stories of our times, (documented in two excellent books, *Our Stolen Future* by Theo Colborn, and *The Feminisation of Nature* by Deborah Cadbury) leading scientists from many disciplines have come to the same conclusions.

We've released chemicals throughout the world that are having fundamental effects on the reproductive system and immune system in wildlife and humans,' says Professor Louis Guillette from the University of Florida.

We have unwittingly entered the ultimate Faustian bargain . . . in return for all the benefits of our modern society, and all the amazing products of modern life, we have more testicular cancer and more breast cancer. We may also affect the ability of the species to reproduce,' says Devra Lee Davis, former deputy health policy advisor to the American government.

They and countless other scientists have come to the

conclusion that a growing number of commonly occurring chemicals, found in our air, water and food, are disrupting hormone balances and acting as carcinogens: these include some pesticides, plastics, industrial compounds and pharmaceutical drugs (see Chapter 15 for more on these).

Most of these chemicals mimic the role in the body of oestrogen, which is a hormone that stimulates the growth of hormone-sensitive tissue. They are classified as xenoestrogens (meaning oestrogenic compounds from outside, as opposed to inside, our bodies). When taken in on top of the natural oestrogen produced by both men and women, plus the added oestrogen taken in by women on the pill or HRT, these chemicals can 'over-oestrogenise' a person.

Too much oestrogen stimulates the excessive proliferation of hormone-sensitive tissue, thus increasing the risk of hormone-related cancers. However, the effect of these substances is not quite so linear. They may also alter genes or promote the expression of oncogenes (see Chapter 5). Essentially, they confuse the hormonal messages the body sends out, changing sexual and reproductive development. They are best thought of as hormone-disrupters, interfering with the body's ability to adapt and respond appropriately to its environment.

Pesticides

Researchers are currently trying to measure the effects of global pollution by such chemicals. In animal studies, exposure to many of these pesticides induces breast cancer[9] and promotes the growth of tumours.[10] Breast cancer mortality in pre-menopausal women dropped by 30 per cent following the implementation of regulations reducing levels of carcinogenic pesticides.[11] Higher levels of DDT and PCBs have been found in human breast cancer tissue compared to healthy tissue.[12] Many other pesticides are known to be carcinogenic, although not necessarily by acting as hormone-disrupters (these are discussed more fully in Chapter 15). With the average person having up to a gallon of pesticides sprayed on the fruit and vegetables they eat each year, the link between cancer and pesticide exposure definitely needs further research.

Plastics

Even more insidious is the potential effect of the hormone-disrupting chemicals found in plastics. One carcinogen found by chance is a component used in plastic to protect it from oxidation. Researchers studying breast cancer cells that had been placed in a plastic container couldn't understand why they were growing so prolifically, as if exposed to oestrogen. It turned out that nonylphenols were leaching from the plastic and having an oestrogenic effect.[13]

Nonylphenol is a proven oestrogen-like agent commonly found in plastic; it can and does leach out of plastic products into food, especially fatty foods (like cheese or crisps) It is also used in products such as spermicides in condoms and gels used with diaphragms. Many detergents and toiletries also contain nonylphenols and they are used as pesticides. They are classified as 'surfectants' so check the products you buy. As many as 18,000 tons of nonylphenols are produced each year in the UK and some end up in our water supply. It is this factor that is believed to be causing the infertility and feminising of fish in polluted rivers.

Based on the evidence to date, it would seem prudent to limit exposure of food, especially fatty foods, to plastic. But this is not as easy as it sounds: plastic packaging is used for most foods, including snacks. Fatty snacks (like crisps) and fatty foods wrapped in clingfilm are on the 'suspect list'. But plastic in food packaging isn't always obvious. For instance, there is a layer of plastic inside many cans and cartons used for drinks. And those that aren't lined may leach dioxins (equally toxic agents used in bleaching paper and card).

Dioxins, which are used as pesticides as well as bleaching agents and in other industrial chemical processes, are not oestrogen-mimickers; yet, through some action we don't yet understand, they feminise male rodents both physically and behaviourally. Dioxins are a by-product of chlorine compounds. Like organochlorines, they are non-biodegradable, and therefore tend to accumulate in the environment.

Environmental groups have been campaigning for legislation to ban nonylphenols and dioxins, to decrease our environmental load, but it is almost certain that other chemicals used in plastic production are also oestrogen-mimickers. Perhaps most concerning is the finding that 'acceptable' levels of a number of chemicals can, in combination, produce a vastly exaggerated oestrogen effect. As each new piece is fitted into the chemical jigsaw, the extent to which we may need to clean up the environment, industrial processing and the food chain becomes clearer.

Such worldwide increased exposure to these hormone disrupters is even more worrying in the light of the finding that a very small change in hormone exposure during foetal development sets a clock ticking for increased cancer risk in adulthood. In other words, over-exposure to these chemicals could be programming us for extinction.

Synthetic hormones, HRT and the Pill

Oestrogens make things grow. And too many oestrogens can promote hormone-sensitive cancers. One study showed that when oestrogen levels were increased in pre-menopausal women with breast lumps, the proliferation rate of breast epithelial cells (those lining the breast) increased by over 200 per cent – more than twice the normal rate. Oestrogen is usually kept in check by progesterone, another hormone produced by the ovaries, which has an anti-proliferation effect. According to the researchers (Dr Chang and colleagues from the National Taiwan University Hospital in Taipei), if natural progesterone is given and the level in breast tissue is raised to normal physiological levels, cell multiplication rate falls to 15 per cent of that in women who have not been treated. So oestrogen promotes the proliferation of breast cancers, while progesterone is protective.[14]

Dr John Lee, from California, a medical expert in female hormones and health, believes:

> The major cause of breast cancer is unopposed oestrogen and there are many factors that would lead to this. Stress, for example, raises cortisol and competes with progesterone for receptor sites. Xenoestrogens from the environment have the ability to damage tissue and lead to an increased risk of cancer later in life. There are also clearly nutritional and genetic factors to consider. What is most concerning is that doctors continue to prescribe unopposed oestrogen to women.

He is, of course, referring to the widespread prescribing of synthetic hormones in contraceptive pills and HRT. The increasing use of synthetic hormones in medicine has been mirrored by the rise in hormone-related cancers.

There could be no more dramatic example of the danger of altering our exposure to these powerful hormone-disrupters than DES, the first synthetic oestrogen, created by Dr Charles Dodds in 1938. Within 20 years, DES was being given to women and to animals. For the latter it improved growth rates, while for women it apparently promised a trouble-free pregnancy and healthier offspring. Eventually, up to six million mothers and babies were exposed to DES.

It wasn't until 1970 that the flaws surfaced. Girls, whose mothers had been on DES during pregnancy, started to show genital development abnormalities and a substantial increase in cancer rates, especially vaginal cancer of a kind never seen before.[15] Then it was discovered that boys whose mothers had taken DES also had defects in the development of their sexual organs.[16] Many DES children died and many more were infertile.

DES is no longer prescribed, but synthetic oestrogens and progestins are, and both are associated with increased cancer risk. A study by Dr Bergvist and colleagues in Scandinavia showed that if a woman is on HRT for longer than five years she doubles her risk of breast cancer.[17] They also found that if the HRT included progestins, the synthetic versions of natural progesterone, that risk was even higher. A large-scale study, published in the *New England Journal of Medicine* in 1995, showed that post-menopausal women who had been on HRT for five or more years had a 71 per cent increased risk of breast cancer.[18] The risk was found to increase with the length of time on HRT. Overall, there was a 32 per cent higher risk among women using oestrogen HRT, and a 41 per cent higher risk for those using oestrogen and synthetic progestin HRT, compared to women who had never used synthetic hormones. An analysis of the results of 51 clinical studies published in *The Lancet* medical journal, involving over 160,000 women, concluded that there was an increased risk of breast cancer in women using HRT; that the risk rises as the duration of use lengthens; and that the risk is reduced once HRT has been stopped.[19]

Breast cancer isn't the only concern. A study in 1995 carried out by the Emery University School for Public Health, followed 240,000 women for eight years and found that the risk of ovarian cancer was 72 per cent higher in women given oestrogen.[20] Another study showed that women using combined oestrogen and cyclic progestagen on a long-term basis had a higher risk of endometrial cancer than those not on hormone replacement. When women used natural oestrogen and progestin, however, the risk was statistically insignificant.[21]

The danger of using synthetic hormones doesn't just lie in the subtle differences in their chemical structure and effect, but also in the amounts given and their balance with other hormones. The amounts of hormones in a contraceptive pill or HRT treatment can be many times higher than the body would naturally produce. Oestrogen produced by the body is balanced with progesterone but, if this balance is lost, oestrogen unopposed by progesterone becomes a health problem.

Dr John Lee, who pioneered the use of natural progesterone, delivered in normal physiological doses in transdermal cream to counteract unopposed oestrogen, has treated over 4000 women with a diagnosis of breast cancer. He says, 'Not one has had a recurrence. Of the tens of thousands of women using progesterone for other reasons not one has called to say they have breast cancer following the use of natural progesterone cream. Natural progesterone is completely safe, and beneficial to give to women with breast cancer.' He also recommends eating a plant-based diet, excluding sources of oestrogens from meat and milk, and supplementing anti-oxidant nutrients including vitamins C and E.

OTHER SOURCES OF OESTROGEN

While men are not exposed to oestrogen compounds from taking the Pill and HRT, their oestrogen load may come from xenoestrogens, oestrogens in food and the small amount of oestradiol produced in a man's body. These oestrogenic chemicals interfere with the male hormone testosterone, preventing it from being active. Also, older men do produce relatively more 'female' hormones later in life. The net effect is to 'oestrogenise' men, increasing the associated risks of getting prostate cancer and other hormone-related cancers.

Dietary oestrogens

We also take in oestrogens from 'natural' foods. Meat, for example, contains significant amounts of oestrogen, as does dairy produce, although the high levels in these foods may indicate that they aren't perhaps as natural as we would like to believe. Much of the meat we eat comes from animals whose feed has hormones added to it. This, coupled with a high protein intake, artificially increases the growth of the animal, which means more profit. Changes in farming practice now make it possible to milk cows continuously, even while they are pregnant. But during pregnancy oestrogen concentrations in milk go up. While calves may benefit from this extra oestrogen, we do not.

Meat and dairy products are also a storage site for non-degradable toxins which accumulate along the food chain. Millions of tons of chemicals, like non-biodegradable PCBs and DDT, have been released into the environment. Traces are found in meat, fish and fowl, which have fed on other animals, which in turn have fed on pastures or in water contaminated with these non-degradable chemicals. These accumulate in their fat and when we eat such fat they accumulate in us.

Plant oestrogens may be protective

Plants also contain natural, oestrogen-like compounds, known as phyto-oestrogens. These are found in a wide variety of foods, including soya, citrus fruits, wheat, licorice, alfalfa, celery and fennel. The richest source is soya and its by-products, such as tofu and soya milk. However, unlike oestrogenic chemicals such as PCBs, these phyto-oestrogens are associated with a reduced risk of cancer. A high dietary intake of isoflavonoids, the active ingredient in soya, is associated with a halving of breast cancer in animals, and a substantial reduction in deaths from prostate cancer in men.[22] Even more encouraging are animal studies which show that eating a small amount of isoflavones in early infancy results in a 60 per cent reduced risk for breast cancer later in life.[23]

The likely explanation for the protective effect of these

oestrogen-like compounds is that they may block the action of other more toxic environmental oestrogens, perhaps by occupying the oestrogen receptor sites on cells. Since they are about a hundred times weaker in their oestrogen effect than xenoestrogens or the body's oestrogen, the net effect of eating foods rich in phyto-oestrogens seems to be to lower the body's oestrogen load and protect us against harmful hormone-disrupting chemicals.

AVOIDING THE HORMONE-DISRUPTERS

Why, you may ask, don't we just do the research to identify which chemicals are causing cancer and ban them? According to Dr Samuel Epstein, Professor of Occupational and Environmental Medicine at the School of Public Health, University of Illinois Medical Centre, Chicago:

> Most of the money [for cancer research] has been squandered on a search for 'cures'; virtually nothing has been done to prevent exposure to carcinogenic chemicals in the environment, despite overwhelming evidence that contamination of our air, water and food is a major cause of cancer. Unfortunately the 'Cancer Establishment' is controlled by the very industries that generate such contaminants. This is the problem that must be addressed if we are to wage a genuine and successful war on cancer.[24]

His words are echoed by Professor Louis Guillette from the University of Florida: 'Should we change policy? Should we be upset? I think we should be fundamentally upset. I think we should be screaming in the streets.' Yet, the reality – until large-scale government action is taken – is that it isn't easy to eliminate all these substances because they are all around us, in our food, water, air and household products. There are, however, steps you can take to substantially reduce your own and your family's exposure (see Chapter 15).

CHAPTER 4

CARCINOGENS IDENTIFIED

We live in a chemical world. Without realising it, we are all exposed to over 10,000 man-made chemicals, an increasing number of which are being identified as carcinogens – i.e. potentially cancer-causing. As the American Chemical Society catalogues the ten millionth man-made chemical, it is becoming increasingly clear that only a minority of these substances are ever thoroughly tested by independent scientists. There are 3500 chemical food additives, of which we eat, on average, 16lb in a year. There's a similar quantity of chemicals in our homes – in household products, toiletries and detergents; and many more in our environment, contaminating our air, water and food. The US Environmental Protection Agency estimated that in 1991 US industries discharged 3.6 billion pounds of chemicals, including a wide range of carcinogens, into the environment.

Few, if any, of these man-made chemicals have been thoroughly investigated for their individual or combined long-term effects on health. Many chemicals to which we are exposed greatly multiply the toxic effects of others, rendering an otherwise 'safe' exposure unsafe.[25] According to a report published back in 1971 by the Massachusetts Institute of Technology (MIT), 'Man's Impact on the Global Environment': 'Synergistic effects among chemical pollutants are more often present than not.' For example, the liver damage caused by small amounts of the solvent carbon tetra-chloride is greatly increased by a small amount of DDT; while its effects are increased a hundredfold if the common drug phenobarbital is added to the cocktail.

POLLUTION

Professor Samuel Epstein, from the School of Public Health, University of Illinois Medical Centre, Chicago, believes the impact of our massive increased exposure to carcinogenic chemicals is very downplayed by the cancer institutions, many of which have close links to the pharmaceutical and chemical industries. He believes our failure to reverse the cancer epidemic is a direct consequence of political decisions which have allowed only a fraction of cancer research to investigate true causes and means of prevention. The major-ity of funds have instead been channelled towards developing a 'cure', in the form of highly profitable medical treatments. Professor Epstein's research suggests that the prevention spot-light has been solely focused on diet and smoking, while allowing the chemical industries to keep making profits and keep polluting our environment. Prevention has been inter-preted to mean early detection, followed by chemotherapy, surgery or radiation, rather than true prevention which means identifying the cause of cancer and eliminating it in the first place.

There are enough holes in cancer statistics to support Epstein's views. Take lung cancer, for example. While no-one questions that smoking is a major causative factor for lung cancer, this doesn't explain how the incidence in non-smokers has doubled over recent decades and is still on the increase. Pollution, especially exhaust fumes and occupational exposure, is almost certainly playing a role. The National Institute for Occupational Safety and Health has estimated that approximately 11 million workers in the US are exposed to occupational carcinogens. The figure in the UK is likely to be in the order of two million.

Pesticides

One group of workers at risk are farmers, even though they are usually considered to be healthier, tend to smoke less, have generally healthier diets and get plenty of exercise. Yet, in the last several decades, farmers have experienced higher than average rates of leukaemia, non-Hodgkin's lymphoma and cancers of the brain and prostate. In animal studies these cancers have been linked to pesticide exposure. These are discussed more fully in Chapter 15.

TELEVISIONS AND COMPUTERS

Many people these days use a VDU screen at work and possibly at home. VDU screens generate an electrostatic field which attracts dust particles towards the screen or the operator's face. This can lead to irritation of the eyes, a runny nose and dry and itchy skin rashes.

This effect reduces rapidly with distance so there is not normally any problem watching the most common type of VDU (i.e. the television screen) unless a person sits right up close to the set. Children should therefore be discouraged from sitting close up to the television.

When operating computers though, a person sits much closer to the screen and prolonged exposure might cause health problems. One way of reducing the problem is to fit an electrically grounded filter in front of the screen. Such devices dramatically reduce the movement of particles towards the operator, though they do not greatly screen out the radiation emitted from the screen. This radiation, however, is not ionising radiation and is not thought to be so much of a health hazard.

LOW-LEVEL RADIATION

Low-level radiation is a factor that is often downplayed. There is no question that radiation is a carcinogen. Rather, the question is, what level of exposure makes a difference and what part is radiation playing in the cancer equation? Since the time lag between carcinogen exposure and cancer can be 15 to 20 years, the almost worldwide increase in cancer incidence in the mid-1970s could point to the release of a new carcinogen between 1955 and 1960. This coincides with the start of nuclear bomb testing. At the peak of testing, concerns were raised about the level of radioactive strontium-90 in milk. (The consumption of milk, potentially contaminated with strontium-90 from fall-out on pastures, tends to be highest among nursing mothers.)

According to Dr Chris Busby of the Low-Level Radiation Campaign, 'Nursing mothers exposed at the peak of testing, who received the largest dose from strontium-90, had the largest increase in breast cancer.' He believes that low-level radiation exposure may also explain why areas in the UK with the highest rainfall, where nuclear fallout would be expected to be higher, first began to show increases in cancer incidence. For example, in 1987 the rate for all cancers was 54 per cent higher in Wales than in East Anglia.

While the birth of the nuclear industry added a new and powerful carcinogen – ionising radiation – the growth of the telecommunications industry exposes all of us to non-ionising radiation from the signals of TVs, radios and mobile phones; and there are microwave ovens too. While assumed to be harmless, evidence is continuing to grow that exposure to certain types of non-ionising radiation, including mobile phones, may be adding to our risk of getting cancer.

Radiation doesn't just come from man-made sources, such as nuclear power generation and medical X-rays. We are all exposed to radiation from the sun and deep space. There are even naturally occurring radioactive materials in our air, food and water. The average person in the UK receives about 87 per cent of their annual radiation dose from natural sources and 11.5 per cent from medical X-rays. The remaining 1.5 per cent comes from artificial non-medical sources, like nuclear power generation – unless something goes wrong, as it did at Chernobyl. (Radiation is discussed more fully in Chapter 13.)

RADON GAS

One of the largest 'natural' sources of radiation is radon gas and most human exposure occurs indoors. Radon gas is produced by uranium as it decays to become lead. Uranium and radium are found naturally in rocks and soil and also in building materials such as wood, bricks and concrete. When the decay products (contained in small dust particles) are inhaled, the radioactive particles settle in the lungs and irradiate intensely at close range for many years.

In the open air any radon is mixed and diluted with air and quickly dispersed. However, indoors, radon particles released from building materials, and from the ground, are inhaled by the occupants.

Recent surveys carried out in the UK suggest that residents in some parts of the country are at greater risk than others. The south-west seems to be the most affected area but other local 'hot spots' have been identified. Areas with high granite are the most affected. In some cases the radiation dose from radon accounts for over 50 per cent of total natural radiation. At this level it is suggested that it could be responsible for about 500 deaths from cancer per year. If you live in a high granite area contact your local Environmental Health Officer to find out what your radon exposure is likely to be. When radon levels are high it is better to use certain building materials than others. Adequate ventilation under floorboards is also important, to remove the radioactive compounds before they can build up to significant levels.

NATURAL CARCINOGENS

Not all carcinogens are man–made. Many carcinogenic chemicals occur in nature and come to us through natural food. These include psoralens, found in parsnips and celery, mycotoxins from moulds found in cheese, milk and bread, and aflatoxins found in some peanuts. In rare cases, when dietary consumption of a natural carcinogen has been excessive, high incidences of cancer have resulted. This occurred in a rural area of China, where the combination of widespread selenium deficiency due to poor soil levels, and the consumption of a type of pickled cabbage (found to be high in the carcinogen nitrosamine), resulted in a high incidence of oesophageal cancer. This was effectively eliminated by enriching the soil with selenium and staying off the pickled cabbage.

However, it is surely beyond the bounds of possibility to suggest that the massive escalation of cancer over the past 30 years is solely a result of people eating more blue cheese or parsnips. Having said that, it is wise to limit consumption of foods potentially high in natural carcinogens by not eating them daily, and probably not more than two or three times a week.

How we process foods and what we add to them is of greater concern. Some permitted food additives are carcinogenic, depending on the dose and which other chemicals they are combined with. These include butylated hydroxy-anisole (E320) which interacts with nitrates to form chemicals known to cause changes in the DNA of cells; potassium nitrate (E249) which is used as a preservative in cured and canned meats; and saccharin, which the International Agency for Research on Cancer believes is possibly carcinogenic to humans. Any fried, burnt or browned food – which means the food has been oxidised – adds to the carcinogenic load of a meal. This applies to a lot of fast food such as French fries, charred burgers, fried fish and crispy pizzas – the staple diet of the younger generation.

In summary, there is no doubt that a major cause of cancer is our increased exposure to carcinogens. Some of these act as oxidants and some as hormone-disrupters, while some damage genes and alter cell behaviour. We can avoid or, at least, substantially reduce our exposure to many of them (see Chapter 17).

CHAPTER 5

IN THE GENES?

Cancer is a genetic disease. The changes that occur in cells seem to be the direct result of mutations or changes to genes. The genes are like the software that tells the molecules in your body – the hardware components – how to organise themselves. Genes interact with the environment: when that interaction goes seriously wrong, cancer results. Genes and environment are interdependent, like the chicken and the egg.

Some scientists argue that genes play a more significant role in cancer than environmental factors, like food, chemical carcinogens and smoking. But if cancer is primarily genetic, why did it emerge as a major cause of death only with industrialisation? There are two possible answers. One is that there have always been people who were genetically predisposed to cancer but that the gene is only 'activated' by exposure to carcinogens. The other is that genetic predisposition to cancer plays a very small part in the overall picture. Both are true.

Some people carry defective genes that cause cells to misbehave. These are called oncogenes. Two oncogenes for breast cancer have been discovered – they are called BRCA1 and BRCA2 and are estimated to be carried by one in 200 women. It is thought that a small percentage of women with breast cancer have, as a contributory factor, the inheritance of such oncogenes.

It is, however, unlikely that just having the oncogene is enough to trigger breast cancer. One survey of women with the BRCA1 gene found that they were actually no more likely to die of the cancer than women with the disease who did not have this gene. The researchers suggested that, by making certain dietary and lifestyle choices, women carrying the gene did not need to resign themselves to contracting fatal cancer.[26] This is because most oncogenes only release their disruptive instructions when activated by carcinogens.

To illustrate how this works, consider the example of the chemical 'nonylphenol' found in paints, detergents, lubricating oils, toiletries, spermicide foams, agrochemicals and many other products.

Inside our cells are receptors for hormones (see Figure 4). The hormone fits like a 'key' into the receptor 'lock'. If the key fits, specific genes are activated, starting a particular biological programme. 'Fake' hormones – or substances which can act like hormones (such as nonylphenols) – are like wonky keys. They can activate genes, but not necessarily the right ones, perhaps triggering an oncogene; so they change the way our biology works. Nonylphenol is known as an 'oestrogen-mimicker' and, like oestrogen itself, can change the programming of the body's biochemistry, depending on how much and what else the cells are exposed to.

The soya bean also contains an oestrogen-like molecule. However, in this case, it seems to bind to oestrogen receptors and stop harmful substances like nonylphenols from perverting the course of genetic expression. So, if anything, it helps to balance hormones; while substances like nonylphenols disturb normal hormone balance.

Such substances are thought to disrupt the body's biochemistry because of their ability to lock onto hormone receptor sites. This alters the ability of genes to communicate with the body's cells (a process known as gene expression), which is vital for our health. In some cases these chemicals

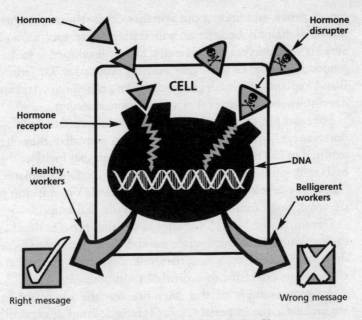

Figure 4 – How hormones and chemicals affect genes

actually block a hormone receptor; in other cases they act as if they were the hormone; while some simply disrupt the hormone message. If you think of this 'hormone – hormone receptor – gene expression – biochemical response' sequence as 'communication', what these chemicals do is turn the sound up or down and scramble the message.

This information is, of course, good news, in that it means the few people who do carry oncogenes (which increase their chances of developing cancer) can counteract this by avoiding carcinogens and increasing their intake of cancer-protective nutrients to suppress the activation of these genes. Such testing, both to determine whether a person has inherited certain oncogenes, and whether or not those oncogenes have been activated, has recently become available (see Useful Addresses) in both the US and UK. Being able to test for cancer genes, and finding out whether or not those genes are active, is helpful because it will enable more specific and personalised prevention strategies to be developed.[27] In his pioneering book *Genetic Nutritioneering* biochemist Dr Jeffrey Bland explains how such genetic profiling is helping scientists develop more effective cancer prevention strategies.

For example, there is a strain of mice predisposed to develop skin cancer due to an inherited gene, provided they are exposed to UVB radiation. However, if their diet includes the herb milk thistle, a rich source of the anti-oxidant silymarin, they don't develop skin cancer.[28] In this case UVB radiation is the triggering carcinogen and silymarin the antidote.

Of course, the biotech industry have other plans in mind as their solution is to manipulate the defective gene with gene therapy. This, of course, carries unknown risks and is certainly more expensive than nutrition solutions.

A great example of this dilemma was the discovery by researchers at the Imperial Cancer Research Fund of a specific oncogene in mice that resulted in them being unable to detoxify smoke. These genetically susceptible mice had a higher risk of developing cancer because the gene in question is partially responsible for making the anti-oxidant enzyme glutathione transferase. According to newspaper reports, a gene pill for people with this defective gene may be available in ten years. Yet the body's ability to make more glutathione transferase is dependent on the protein glutathione and the mineral selenium – which are both widely deficient among British people. An alternative to gene manipulation would be to ensure an optimal intake of these nutrients.

In summary, genetic predisposition to cancer plays a very small role in the major cancers of the late 20th century. In any event, they are likely to require activation by avoidable carcinogens and can be effectively left 'dormant' by ensuring optimal intakes of key nutrients. Part 4 explains exactly how to do this.

CHAPTER 6

HOW STRONG ARE YOUR IMMUNE DEFENCES?

As well as being a disease of the genes, cancer is an immune disease. It is the immune system's job to hunt around the body, identify pre-cancerous cells and put them out of action. This happens in each of us every single day.

However, if a person's immune defences are weak, pre-cancerous cells can multiply, possibly resulting in some form of cancer. An example of this is HIV infection. The virus responsible for AIDS selectively destroys immune cells, leaving the body without its usual defences. The incidence of one type of cancer, Karposi's sarcoma, is consequently high in people with AIDS.

Until recently, the accepted method of dealing with immune-related diseases was always to kill the invader, be it a bacteria, virus or cancer cell. This approach is, however, becoming less popular because of the high cost of combative drugs. An alternative strategy is to support the body's own immune system. A new class of cancer drug works on this basis: 'monoclonal antibodies,' for example, target cancer cells for non-Hodgkin's lymphoma, tagging them so that the body's own immune system sees them clearly and moves in for the kill.

You can also boost your immune system without drugs. The immune system depends on a whole host of nutrients, and supplementing these has been proven to enhance immunity.

This approach – of also boosting immunity, rather than just focusing on killing the invader – is likely to prove much more effective. After all, we have achieved vast improvements in sanitation in the Western world this century, yet, in the last 20 years, medicine has doled out billions of antibiotic, anti-viral and anti-fungal medicines. If the invader-killing approach was working you'd expect fewer overall deaths from infections. In fact exactly the opposite has occurred.

In both the US and the UK the number of infections has increased dramatically. A survey of all deaths in the US between 1980 and 1992 revealed an alarming 58 per cent rise in deaths from infectious diseases.[29] A six-fold increase occurred in those between the ages of 25 and 44. This is only partly due to the increased number of deaths from HIV infection. Deaths from respiratory infections increased by 20 per cent. And the same trends can be seen in Britain.[30]

According to Spence Galbraith, former director of the Communicable Diseases Surveillance Centre,[31] 'The rate of change of human infection appears to be increasing. It is now recognised that it can only be a matter of time until the next microbial menace to our species emerges amongst us.' Coupled with the increased risk of cancer, this global trend suggests that our immune defences aren't as strong as they should be.

HOW DOES YOUR IMMUNE SYSTEM WORK?

Before discussing ways of boosting the immune system, we need a brief description of the 'immune army' and its role.

Immunological battles can occur anywhere in the body – against invading organisms or against our own rebellious cells (as in cancer). To fight off these enemies, we have a fixed defence framework, called the lymphatic system (shown in Figure 5), which works alongside other parts of the body, such as the bone marrow, thymus and spleen. The complex workings of the immune system are largely controlled by the pituitary and adrenal glands.

The blood plays a vital role in our defences. Made up of a clear yellow fluid (called plasma) and blood cells which are suspended in the fluid, our blood provides us with a mobile fighting force of white blood cells (or leukocytes) which are our main immune soldiers. When our systems are in good working order, we can produce around 2000 new immune cells every second. These white blood cells are present in lymph as well as in the blood.

There are three main types of white blood cell: granulocytes, monocytes and lymphocytes. Most of the granulocytes are phagocytic (which means that they gobble up any foreign bacteria they come across). Monocytes or macrophages perform a crucial 'cleaning' role, eating anything that is rubbish or foreign, and cleaning our blood, tissues and lymph. They are also major 'armament factories', capable of making at least 40 different enzymes and immune proteins needed to destroy enemies.

Finally, lymphocytes are the most competent and versatile group of cells for getting rid of 'unwanted guests'. Some of them have a memory system, so that they recognise a bug which has previously attacked the body, and thus trigger the immune system to fight back straight away. Lymphocytes also have a special method of dividing rapidly when they are under attack, producing reinforcements almost immediately. This rapid division is very nutrient-dependent – for example, vitamin C levels are crucial. The three types of lymphocytes are T-cells and B-cells and natural killer (NK) cells. The latter are particularly important as they seek and destroy cancer cells.

T-cells regulate the immune system and decide whether it should go into battle or withdraw. They provide the initial response to viruses and tumour cells. But it takes three or four days after recognition of these for the T-cells to get their act together and attack.

B-cells deal mainly with bacteria and viruses that have been encountered before. A B-cell takes an invading bug into the tissues, where it ascertains its exact size and shape. It then tailor-makes a protein 'straitjacket' (called an antibody) that will fit that bug and no other. Finally, it gets a production line going to manufacture thousands more of these antibodies which are released back into the body. The antibodies seek out their targets like mini guided missiles and attach themselves to the bacteria. The invader becomes harmless and is held until the macrophages come along to devour it.

BOOSTING YOUR IMMUNE SYSTEM

The idea that people may be prone to cancer partly because of immune deficiency is largely uncharted territory as far as cancer research is concerned. However, we do know which nutrients boost immunity (the ones which tend to be low in those who succumb to cancer) and which nutrients aid recovery. This whole area of optimum nutrition and its role in boosting immunity and preventing cancer is covered in detail in Part 2. But, at this stage, we can say that deficiencies in the following nutrients increase a person's risk of developing this disease:

Vitamin A is especially important because it helps to maintain the integrity of the digestive tract, lungs and all cell membranes, preventing foreign agents from entering the body, and preventing viruses from entering cells. In addition, vitamin A and beta-carotene (its vegetable form) are potent anti-oxidants; many foreign agents produce free oxidising radicals (oxidants) as part of their defence system. Macrophages also produce free radicals to destroy invaders. A high intake of anti-oxidant nutrients helps to protect immune cells from these harmful weapons. The ideal intake of beta-carotene is between 10,000iu (3300mcgRE) and 30,000iu (10,000mcgRE) per day.

Vitamin B5, B6, B12 and folic acid are all important to the immune system. The production of antibodies and the function of T-lymphocytes depend on B6, so it is essential when fighting cancer cells. The ideal daily intake is 50–100mg. B12 and folic acid are also important for the same reasons. The ideal daily intake is 100mcg for B12 and 400mcg for folic acid. Pantothenic acid (B5) helps macrophages and natural killer cells do their job, while deficiency is associated with inhibition of T-cell and antibody production. The ideal daily intake is 100–300mg.

Vitamin C is unquestionably the most vital immune-boosting nutrient, with more than a dozen proven immune-boosting roles – including production of T-cells which destroy cancer cells. The right dosage is essential. During a viral infection, saturation with vitamin C prevents viruses from multiplying. This usually involves daily doses of 10g or more, spread throughout the day. That's more than 100 times the RDA! Fortunately, vitamin C is one of the least toxic substances known to man. Otherwise, it's ideal to take up to 1000mg daily.

Vitamin E is another important all-rounder. It improves B- and T-cell function and is a powerful anti-oxidant. Its immune-boosting properties increase when given in conjunction with selenium. The ideal daily intake is between 400 and 800iu.

Selenium, manganese, copper and zinc are all involved in anti-oxidation and have all been shown to enhance immunity. Of these, selenium and zinc are the most important. Zinc is critical for immune cell production and function of B- and T-cells that tag and destroy cancer. Selenium boosts immunity and works synergistically with vitamin E. Ideal daily doses are 100–200mcg. The ideal daily intake for zinc is 15–35mg.

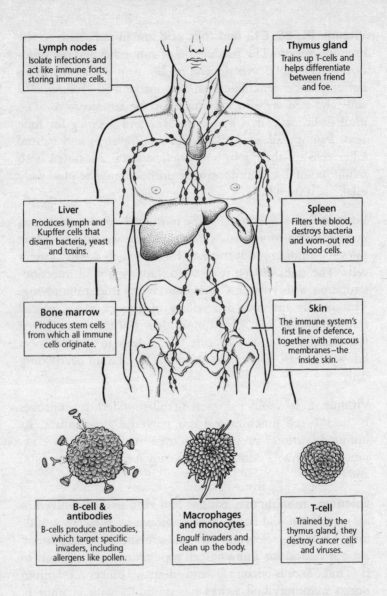

Lymph nodes
Isolate infections and act like immune forts, storing immune cells.

Thymus gland
Trains up T-cells and helps differentiate between friend and foe.

Liver
Produces lymph and Kupffer cells that disarm bacteria, yeast and toxins.

Spleen
Filters the blood, destroys bacteria and worn-out red blood cells.

Bone marrow
Produces stem cells from which all immune cells originate.

Skin
The immune system's first line of defence, together with mucous membranes – the inside skin.

B-cell & antibodies
B-cells produce antibodies, which target specific invaders, including allergens like pollen.

Macrophages and monocytes
Engulf invaders and clean up the body.

T-cell
Trained by the thymus gland, they destroy cancer cells and viruses.

Figure 5 – The immune system

Calcium is needed for the immune cells to produce enzymes to knock out cancer cells.

Cysteine is very important for the immune system, mainly because it is turned into glutathione in the body. When we are exposed to toxins, provided there is sufficient cysteine present, the body can increase its levels of glutathione to detoxify them. High cysteine levels are associated with longevity and reduced cancer risk. In chronic infections such as AIDS, depletion of glutathione is a major concern. Glutathione is vital for macrophages to make the chemicals they need to kill invaders, for lymphocyte production and for red blood cell membranes. It is also critical for the function of natural killer cells. Good sources of cysteine are meat, eggs, soya, quinoa (a grain that cooks like rice), seeds, nuts, onions and garlic. It can be supplemented as n–acetyl cysteine, at 500mg a day.

Other anti-oxidants

There are many other important anti–oxidants not classified as essential vitamins, minerals or amino acids. Some are, however, very important in boosting the immune system and protecting against cancer. Of particular importance are anthocyanidins, which give berries, grapes and beetroot their red/blue colour; co-enzyme Q which helps recycle vitamin E and protects cells from harmful oxidants; and carotenoids, substances related to beta–carotene such as lutein and lycopene, especially rich in cooked tomatoes. Similar to vitamin E (called tocopherol) are tocotrienols, also found in seeds and nuts. As more and more active chemicals are found in natural foods, it is becoming increasingly clear that food is the best medicine of all.

Although some people have attributed their recovery from cancer to dietary changes, nutritional therapy is never claimed to 'cure' cancer. Rather, it can create the best possible conditions within the body for its own anti-cancer mechanisms (primarily the immune system) to restore health. In a healthy individual, cancer is kept at bay by the immune system, which can be very powerful, and is responsible for the natural remissions which can occur in this disease.

It is also possible to stimulate the immune system by means of the appropriate mental attitude (see Chapter 18). Conversely, it is thought that a life-long susceptibility to depression can suppress the immune system and thus weaken a person's defence against cancer and other diseases.

DETOXIFYING CARCINOGENS

One of our key lines of defence is the immune system's ability to detoxify harmful chemicals. Not only do we take in many toxic chemicals, but the body also produces its own. As we process food – turning it into energy or building materials – toxic substances are produced and processed, ready for elimination. This ability to detoxify gives us built-in protection from a certain degree of exposure to toxic substances. This probably explains why mankind has been able to eat natural foods, with their inherent levels of toxic substances, without developing cancer. However, the more toxic substances we are exposed to, the harder the body has to work at detoxifying.

One of the main ways the body neutralises harmful chemicals is to 'package' them ready for export. By sticking harmless molecules onto poisons (in a process called 'conjugation') toxins can be eliminated from the body without doing damage. Of all the building activity that goes on in the body, no less than two-thirds is spent 'conjugating' toxins ready for elimination.

It is highly likely that people prone to cancer have poor detoxification potential either as a result of over-exposure to

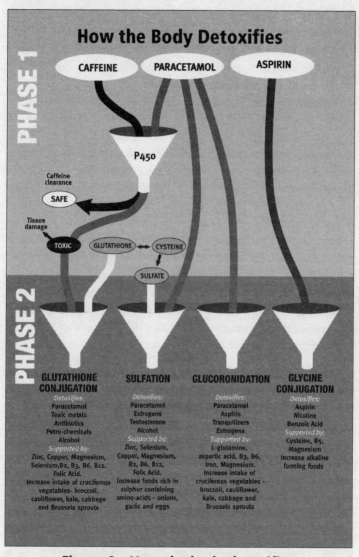

Figure 6 – How the body detoxifies

carcinogens (such as oxidants), or because they have an underlying imbalance – making them more sensitive to carcinogens. Indeed, one of the genes thought to predispose a person to cancer is responsible for making a key detoxifying enzyme called glutathione transferase.

In mice, if you knock out this gene – thus lowering the body's levels of this enzyme – and then expose the subjects to cigarette smoke they will rapidly develop lung cancer. While the geneticists scramble to produce a treatment to correct a defective gene, we can already improve the body's levels of glutathione transferase simply by ensuring an adequate intake of glutathione (or its precursor, n-acetyl cysteine), and selenium, which helps the enzyme to work.

Of course, glutathione transferase is only one of many enzymes involved in detoxification. The four main chemical pathways by which the body detoxifies harmful substances are shown in Figure 6. These are completely dependent on a wide range of nutrients, including vitamins, minerals, amino acids and 'phytonutrients' found in foods such as garlic or cruciferous vegetables like broccoli.

VIRUSES AND CANCER

Some rather rare viruses can trigger cancer although they don't appear to do it on their own. For example, Karposi's sarcoma (a cancer that AIDS patients are more likely to develop) is probably not so much caused by the HIV virus itself but rather results from the HIV virus weakening a person's immune system. The papilloma virus is implicated in the majority of cases of cervical cancer, a condition which is also more prevalent among women with many sexual partners. It is not, however, the only cause of the disease. A few other rare viral infections have been linked to rare types of cancer, but again only as part of a larger causative picture. Suffice to say that, in the vast majority of cancers, there is no evidence to suggest that viruses are responsible. In any event, following the advice in this book will help strengthen your immune system and, in so doing, minimise the harmful effects of viruses.

CHAPTER 7

COMMUNICATION
BREAKDOWN

Rather than thinking of cancer as something 'out there' that must be destroyed, we should perhaps see it as the inevitable consequence of a major breakdown in communication.

Genes 'talk' to the chemicals that enter our bodies, telling them how to become incorporated into this highly complex and intelligent structure. The chemicals, in turn, 'talk' to the genes, adapting and altering their expression. If this conversation is harmonious the body's cells continue to work for the good of the whole. On the other hand, if the conversation goes haywire certain cells stop talking to their co-workers, and stop respecting their boundaries and their duties. They then start to multiply, spread and disrupt the integrity of our bodies, i.e. our health.

In most cases this scenario, i.e. cancer, is caused by a number of factors, which can be summarised as follows:

- Excessive exposure to carcinogens, including hormone-disrupting chemicals and oxidants
- Insufficient intake of anti-oxidants
- A weakened immune system
- Decreased ability to detoxify

The relative importance of each of these factors is different for each of us and is certainly different in different kinds of cancer. However, from this perspective you can see more clearly how to prevent cancer. There are four key measures you need to take:

- Reduce your exposure to carcinogens
- Increase your intake of anti-carcinogens (such as anti-oxidants)
- Boost your immune system
- Improve your ability to detoxify carcinogens

When it comes to reversing the cancer process once it has started all these measures are equally important. However there is also a fifth one: creating an environment where it is difficult for the cancer mass to survive. The latest cancer therapies attempt to find more intelligent ways of giving the cancer mass a hard time than conventional surgery, chemotherapy and radiation. These treatments take the form of drugs that target only the cancer cells, or they involve different methods of cutting off a tumour's blood supply. For example, a number of 'anti-angiogenic' drugs and natural agents – that inhibit a tumour's ability to build its own blood supply (angiogenesis) – now exist. Initial results are encouraging.

However, it is a rare cancer specialist who applies these anti-cancer strategies *and* the four key prevention measures. I have often spoken to cancer patients who have had one treatment or another but have never been given any advice about changing their diet or lifestyle. Yet it makes no sense to keep doing the same things and expect different results. Even when a cancer has apparently been successfully treated, if you do not understand and change the circumstances that led to its development in the first place, why should the disease not reoccur?

By all accounts, cancer is the symptom of a disease process that usually begins at least a decade or more before symptoms develop. True cancer prevention should therefore start with making changes to your diet and lifestyle now (instead of when the first signs of a problem appear or at the final hour).

This book draws together the available evidence, and aims to define what you need to eat and how you need to live to minimise your chances of ever developing the crisis of communication in the body known as cancer.

Part 2 looks at what you need to eat and drink, and what you should avoid; Part 3 looks at lifestyle factors and the art of chemical self-defence; and Part 4 examines the benefits of increasing your intake of anti-cancer nutrients and natural remedies. Part 5 puts it all together into a daily action plan that will help you *say no to cancer.*

ANTI-CANCER
FOODS

CHAPTER 8

···

HOW MUCH MEAT IS SAFE
TO EAT?

What you eat provides you with your greatest risk of, or protection from cancer, even greater than stopping smoking. Thanks to the work of the World Cancer Research Fund (WCRF), there are now some very clear indications of how important diet is in cancer prevention. The WCRF painstakingly reviewed thousands of studies investigating the link between diet and cancer risk, and published the findings in a report entitled 'Food, Nutrition and the Prevention of Cancer: a global perspective'. They concluded that by making a few simple changes to your diet you can reduce your risk by 30 to 40 per cent. The first step is to cut right back on meat. Their advice is, 'If eaten at all, [to] limit intake of red meat to less than 80g (3 oz) daily. It is preferable to choose fish, poultry or meat from non-domesticated animals in place of red meat.'

The results of a large-scale study in Britain showed that vegetarians have a fraction of the risk of contracting life-threatening diseases compared to meat-eaters. The study, carried out by Jim Mann from the University of Otago in New Zealand, investigated the diets of 6115 non-meat-eaters in the UK compared to 5015 of their friends and relatives. After the effects of smoking, obesity and social class were taken into account, the death rates from cancer and heart disease over 12 years were substantially lower in vegetarians: cancer incidence was 40 per cent lower in non-meat eaters.[1] These results have been confirmed by others. According to a survey involving nearly 48,000 men, those who ate red meat more than five times a week were 2.6 times more likely to get prostate cancer than those who ate it only once a week.[2]

However, not all studies have confirmed the link between meat and cancer, which, says the WCRF, is strongest for colorectal cancer and evident for breast, prostate, kidney and pancreatic cancer. For example, one study that followed 3660 adults in Britain over a seven-year period found no associations between increased meat consumption and a higher risk of cancer.[3] In the USA, however, there is much stronger evidence that links meat consumption to cancer risk. Why the conflicting findings?

WHAT'S WRONG WITH MEAT?

It may not be meat, per se, that increases risk but what's in meat and what we do to it. One suggestion is that different cooking methods, combined with a low fruit and vegetable intake in the USA, partly explain why findings in the UK and the USA are different. Also, eating a lot of meat means having a high-protein diet. Protein intakes consistent with a 'meat and two veg' diet have been shown to increase the incidence of all types of cancer in animals. The research carried out by Dr Linda Youngman of Oxford University and Dr Campbell from Cornell University in the US confirms other findings linking excess protein to cancer and other diseases. The RDA for protein is 7.5 per cent of calories but most people eat nearly twice that much, says Youngman. 'People would be far more healthy if they trimmed back their protein intake to the RDA.'

A study in Sweden examining the diets of over 700 people did not find a correlation between kidney cancer and meat consumption per se; but the researchers did find an increase in cancer linked to the intake of fried or sautéed meat.[4] The fat in meat, if burnt, generates oxidants and carcinogens. Grilling, broiling, barbecuing and frying meat all increase the risk, particularly of stomach and colorectal cancer. The high saturated fat content of most meats is also a factor (this is discussed more fully in Chapter 10).

It is not surprising to find that a diet of cooked meat, high in protein and fat, and low in fibre, together with carcinogens created from burning, creates havoc with the digestive tract. All this explains the link with cancer of the stomach, colon, rectum and pancreas (the organ responsible for digesting protein). Why, though, the link with breast and prostate cancer?

THE HORMONE CONNECTION

The higher incidence of these hormone-related cancers among meat-eaters suggests that such a diet introduces a different kind of carcinogen that disrupts hormones. One candidate, of course, is simply the naturally occurring hormones in meat. Such hormones are also present in milk products – excessive consumption of these has been linked to an increased risk of cancer of the prostate and kidney. (The kidneys, being organs of elimination, are exposed to toxic substances as they are removed from the body, including the toxic breakdown products of protein.) However, yoghurt protects us against colon cancer, since the bacteria lactobacillus acidophilus (found in many yoghurts) slows down the development of colon tumours, according to research carried out at Tufts University in 1990.[5]

Most non-organic meat today, whether from chicken, beef, pork or lamb, has received hormone treatment of one kind or another. Animals are given hormone pellets to increase their growth or milk yield. And milk is another source of hormones, particularly oestrogen. Of course, it isn't easy to find out what long-term effects these artificially introduced hormones are having.

Dr Malcolm Carruthers, a specialist in male hormone-related disease, investigated, over seven years, 1000 patients complaining of symptoms of the 'male menopause'. The most common symptoms are fatigue, depression, loss of libido, testicular atrophy, impotence, and breast enlargement, plus an increased risk of prostate cancer. Of those 1000 cases, the highest occupational risk group was farmers (the 'front-line' troops in the agrochemical arms race). According to Carruthers, 'For some the causative agent appeared obvious. They had worked on farms caponizing chickens or turkeys with oestrogen pellet implants, to make the birds plumper and more tender. Unfortunately, though it might be considered poetic justice, they must have taken in large amounts of oestrogen which caused them to become partly caponized themselves.' Farmers less directly exposed to hormones and pesticides, both of which are known to interfere with male hormone balance, also had a high risk for 'male menopause' symptoms.

Any normal person might be incensed to find that their food has been tampered with by the profit-greedy agrochemical and food industry, but in some respects Britain is tame in comparison to the US, where many hormones banned in Europe are still widely used. One of these is Bovine Somatotrophin (BST), given to increase milk yield. With world trade legislation increasingly moving towards the removal of trade barriers, the US are putting pressure on EU countries to lift their ban on BST, residues of which can be found in US milk and other dairy products.

As well as the hormones added to stimulate meat and milk production, meat is a potential reservoir for DDT and its breakdown products. One of the most powerful hormone-disrupting chemicals, DDT was widely used as a pesticide from 1939. It was banned in the USA in 1968 and most other countries thereafter. However, it is non-degradable and passes along the food chain to end up stored in fat tissue, which is where the body puts toxins it can't get rid of. Therefore, even today, according to surveys by the Ministry of Agriculture, Food and Fisheries, we may each have as much as a few hundred milligrams of DDT in our bodies.

In summary, the weight of evidence is in favour of decreasing meat intake to reduce cancer risk. Those wishing to maintain optimal health and minimal risk for cancer should follow these guidelines:

- Preferably avoid or, at least, limit your intake of red meat to a maximum of 80g (3 oz) a day.

- Avoid or rarely eat burnt meat, whether grilled, fried or barbecued.

- Choose organic meat or free-range chicken.

- Eat low-fat meat such as chicken or game, in preference to red meat or meat from domesticated animals.

- Limit your intake of dairy food, choosing organic whenever possible.

CHAPTER 9

FRUIT, VEGETABLES AND PHYTONUTRIENTS

Of all the dietary factors, increasing your intake of fruit and vegetables provides the greatest protection from cancer – and there's no cut-off point. In other words, the more of these foods you eat, the lower your risk. According to the World Cancer Research Fund report, 'The implementation of one recommendation – consumption of 400g/day or more of a variety of vegetables and fruits – could, by itself, decrease overall cancer incidence by at least 20 per cent.'

The evidence is equally strong for eating fruits as well as vegetables, and this is why the government encourages us all to eat at least five servings of these foods per day. One study compared people on a Mediterranean diet – high in fruits, vegetables and cereals – with others on a control diet (similar to the American Heart Association's 'prudent' diet for heart disease). After four years those on the Mediterranean diet showed a 61 per cent reduction in cancer risk and a 50 per cent reduced mortality.[6]

The link between increasing intake of fruit and vegetables and decreasing risk is very convincing for cancers of the digestive tract (mouth, pharynx, stomach, colon and rectum). It is also very strong for lung cancer and breast cancer, with some evidence for other hormone-related cancers, as well as cancer of the kidneys. A study in Sweden, looking into the diets of over 700 people, found a positive correlation between fruit intake and a 50 to 60 per cent reduced risk of developing cancer of the kidney.[7]

It was this strong link that led to investigations into what the protective factors in these foods were. Certain foods appear to be especially protective. Among these are carrots – some studies have indicated that one carrot a day could halve risk for lung cancer[8] – and tomatoes. Men consuming at least ten servings of tomato-based foods a week are almost 50 per cent less likely to develop prostate cancer, whereas those consuming four to seven servings a week are only 20 per cent less likely to develop the disease.[9]

ANTI-OXIDANT POWER

Both carrots and tomatoes are high in anti-oxidant nutrients which are known to protect against cancer-causing oxidant damage. While fruits and vegetables are rich in a wide variety of anti-oxidants, the most research has been carried out on the amount of vitamins A and C in foods. The higher a person's intake of vitamin A (or more particularly beta-carotene, the fruit and vegetable source of vitamin A), the lower their risk of lung cancer.

A study in Japan, of 265,000 people, found that those with a low beta-carotene intake had a much higher risk of lung cancer.[10] This was confirmed by a study published in *The Lancet* which showed that a heavy smoker with a high beta-carotene status had the same risk of developing lung cancer as a non-smoker with a low beta-carotene status.[11] This study illustrates just how important both sides of the cancer equation are – exposure to carcinogens (in this case oxidants from smoke) versus protection factors (in this case the anti-oxidant beta-carotene). Carrots, broccoli, sweet potatoes, cantaloupe melons and apricots are particularly high in beta-carotene. Fresh vegetables and fruit are high in vitamin C. Eating these foods appears to prevent DNA damage (stopping the initiation of cancer)[12] and also to stop the cancer developing.[13] The chart below shows which foods are high in these key anti-oxidant nutrients.

Foods Rich in Anti-oxidants

The best all-round anti-oxidant foods have the highest numbers of stars. Foods are listed in order of their star rating. Make sure these foods form a large part of your diet.

Food	Rich Source of A	C	E
Sweet potatoes	★★★	★	★★★
Carrots	★★★	★★★	
Watercress	★★★	★★★	
Peas	★	★★	★★
Broccoli	★★	★★★	
Cauliflower	★	★★★	
Lemons	★	★★★	
Mangoes	★★	★★	
Meat	★★		★★
Melon	★★	★★	
Peppers	★	★★★	
Pumpkin	★★	★★	
Strawberries	★	★★★	
Tomatoes	★★	★★	
Cabbage	★★★		
Grapefruit	★	★★	
Kiwi fruit	★	★★	
Oranges	★	★★	
Seeds and nuts			★★★
Squash	★★★		
Tuna, mackerel, salmon			★★★
Wheatgerm			★★★
Apricots	★★		
Beans			★★

While vitamin A, C and E are very important in preventing cancer (see Chapter 20), it is becoming clear that there is much more to fruit and vegetables than their vitamin content. There are literally hundreds of active compounds in plants, collectively known as phytonutrients (phyto=plant). Many of these active compounds are cancer-protective anti-oxidants.

Among these are nutrients now appearing in nutritional supplements, such as quercitin (from cranberry); rutin (from buckwheat); catechin (from grapes); pycnogenol (from pine bark); silymarin (from milk thistle); bilberry and anthocyanidins (from berries). (Their role as supplements is discussed in more detail in Part 4.) Many of these phytonutrients determine the colour of food. The carotenoids, including beta-carotene, are responsible for the orange colour of carrots, while anthocyanidins give berries their red/blue hue. In general terms there is good reason to recommend, not only eating plenty of fruits and vegetables, but also choosing those that give a good variety of colour, including oranges, blues and reds.

CRUCIFEROUS VEGETABLES – ARE YOU EATING ENOUGH?

Another protective factor in plants is a family of phytonutrients called glucosinolates. These are found particularly in cruciferous vegetables, a family of vegetables whose leaves grow as a cross: broccoli, cabbage, cauliflower, Brussels sprouts, cress, horseradish, kale, kohlrabi, mustard, radish and turnip. Eating cruciferous vegetables three times a week may halve your risk of colon cancer[14] among others. Glucosinolates appear to help detoxify some carcinogens.

In one study, subjects first ate glucosinolate-containing Brussels sprouts for seven days and then glucosinolate-free sprouts for the same period. After the week of glucosinolates, detoxification enzymes in the colon increased by 30 per cent, compared to the glucosinolate-free period.[15] The evidence for their protective effect is not as strong as that for fruits and vegetables high in anti-oxidants. Nevertheless there is increasing evidence that glucosinolates in cruciferous vegetables help us withstand the burden of daily exposure to toxins and carcinogens, by enhancing the body's production of detoxifying enzymes.

Glucosinolates, especially a substance called indole-3-carbinol (I3C), may also help to protect against harmful oxidants and oestrogens in the body.[16] As we have seen, high oestrogen levels are linked with breast and uterine cancer. But oestrogen is generally deactivated by I3C. Animal studies using I3C have shown reduced incidence of cancer.

SOYA AND CANCER PREVENTION

Glucosinolates aren't the only factor in plant food that may protect against hormone-related cancers. Asian people who swap their traditional diets of bean curd and soya milk for burgers and fries are increasing their risk of cancer as well as heart disease. Collaborative research between Hong Kong's Chinese University and Manchester University indicates that soya beans may protect people from developing prostate and breast cancer.

Soya beans contain large amounts of phyto-oestrogens which may have a protective effect. The traditional Oriental diet is particularly high in isoflavonoids, one type of phyto-oestrogen. Levels of isoflavonoids in the blood have been found to be seven to 110 times higher in Japanese men with a low incidence of prostate cancer, compared to Finnish men.[17] However, we still don't understand exactly how phyto-oestrogens help. Professor Sir Norman Blacklock from Manchester University believes they may exert a 'weak oestrogen effect'; and it is thought that phyto-oestrogens may block oestrogen receptor sites, thereby lowering the body's levels of active oestrogen. If this proves to be so, it is consistent with accumulating evidence that many modern diseases, including breast and prostate cancer, are the result of too much oestrogen.

There is also reason to believe that a protease inhibitor in soya, Bowman-Birk Inhibitor (BBI), may be another key anti-cancer compound. In a study at the University of Pennsylvania School of Medicine, BBI was added to the diet of rats that had previously been fed a substance known to induce colon cancer. None of the rats developed tumours. In another similar study, BBI suppressed the formation of tumours by 71 per cent.[18]

Whatever the mechanism, phyto-oestrogens have consistently been associated with reduced cancer risk. Women whose diets are abundant in soya beans have a lower risk of getting breast cancer, while men with a high soya intake have a substantially lower risk of prostate cancer. Research is beginning to focus on two isoflavonoids – genistein and daidzein. Japanese women, who generally have a lower risk of breast cancer than women in other industrialised societies, have been found to have higher levels of these in their bodies. They may protect against the harmful effects of unopposed oestrogen.

One recent study suggested that long-term regular soya intake, which exposes tissues to these two isoflavonoids, enhances their protective effects.[19] And further studies have illustrated the role of other phytonutrients in soya – the isoflavone equol and the lignan enterolactone – in lowering the risk of breast cancer.[20] Researchers also believe that soya beans may offer protection partly by inhibiting the development of new blood vessels, thus starving the tumour of nourishment. Soya may therefore both protect against the initiation of hormone-related cancers and inhibit the development of cancer.

A likely ideal intake for cancer prevention is around 5mg a day of genistein and daidzein, which is equivalent to a 12 oz serving of soya milk or a serving of tofu. Tofu, a curd made from the soya bean, is the richest source of isoflavonoids, while highly processed soya products are the poorest source.[21] Although it will be some years before human trials are completed, there are certainly good grounds for including soya in your anti-cancer diet.[22]

GARLIC AND TURMERIC

Adding garlic and turmeric to your vegetable dishes will add flavour and simultaneously reduce your risk of cancer. Regular consumption of garlic offers protection, particularly against cancers of the digestive system.[23] Garlic contains around 200 biologically active compounds, many of which protect against cancer and heart disease. Turmeric, a yellow spice rich in the phytonutrient curcumin, is a known anti-inflammatory agent and, in animals, inhibits the growth of cancer.[24]

EAT ORGANIC

While there is good reason to be concerned about the use of herbicides and pesticides, the strong worldwide association between eating lots of fruit and vegetables and reduced cancer risk suggests that the positive factors in these foods outweigh any such negative effects. Having said that, eating organic fruit and vegetables (which are cultivated without the use of pesticides and herbicides) may confer extra protection by minimising your exposure to toxins. This is an area that definitely warrants more research. They have also been found to contain, on average, around 50 per cent more minerals.

Of the pesticides and herbicides used in different countries, Lindane, Mirex, 2,4-D and 2,4,5-T are classified as possible human carcinogens. Aldrin, Endrin and Dieldrin are also on the suspect list, based on animal experiments. Many more are known to cause gene damage (see page 100). Although it has now been banned, exposure to the pesticide DDT has been shown to increase risk of breast cancer. DDT is non-biodegradable and residues are still found in food and human tissue.

What is particularly worrying is the evidence that children consume more pesticide residues than adults. This is probably because they eat more fruit and food in general, in relation to their body size, and because pesticide exposure during the 'developing years' significantly increases risk. (The link between pesticide exposure and cancer is discussed further in Chapter 15.)

There is good reason, both from the point of view of cancer risk and general health, to eat organic and feed your children organic fruit and vegetables whenever possible.

In summary, to maximise your protection against cancer:

- Eat as much fruit and vegetables as possible – at least five servings a day.

- Have a variety of 'colours' of fruits and vegetables, including something orange every day (such as carrots, sweet potato, tomatoes, peaches or canteloupe melons) and something red/purple (such as berries, grapes or beetroot).

- Include a serving of cruciferous vegetables every day. These include broccoli, Brussels sprouts, cabbage, cauliflower and kale.

- Eat organic whenever possible.

- Have a clove of garlic a day.

- Have some soya milk, or tofu every other day.

CHAPTER 10

GOOD FATS AND BAD FATS

Our modern diet is too high in fat, which accounts for around 40 per cent of our total calorie intake. The ideal figure is around 20 per cent, with most government targets set at reducing fat intake to 30 per cent. Even more important than the quantity, however, is the *kind* of fat we eat and *how* we eat it.

Too much hard or saturated fat (the type found mainly in meat and dairy products) means a higher risk of cardiovascular disease and is tentatively linked to an increased risk of cancers of the breast, prostate, endometrium (womb) and also colorectal cancer. So say the National Cancer Institute and the WRCF (World Cancer Research Fund). The World Health Organisation's International Agency for Research on Cancer has also reported an association between increased risk for breast cancer – children who eat high fat diets. However, there are many possible interpretations of the data. Since the associated cancers are primarily hormone-related, and since most saturated fat comes from intensively reared animals (often treated with hormones), it may well be that eating a high-fat diet increases a person's exposure to hormone-disrupting chemicals and hormone residues. Also, the higher the percentage of body fat, the more the hormone oestrogen is likely to be stored rather than removed.

Perhaps even more significant is the fact that modern man

is grossly deficient in essential or polyunsaturated fats – found in seeds, nuts, fish and their oils. These essential fats (which come in two families, known as Omega-3 and Omega-6 fats) are vital constituents of a healthy diet; they are unquestionably essential for the immune system and cell health.

While polyunsaturated fats are essential for health, they are also much more prone to damage – to becoming oxidised – than saturated fat. High temperatures or processing can make these good fats bad. Instead of getting our essential fats from raw seeds, nuts and their cold-pressed oils or fish, most of the polyunsaturated fats we take in are already damaged through heating or processing in the form of processed foods, margarine and refined oils used for frying. When coupled with a poor intake of anti-oxidants, this is a recipe for disaster.

Consequently, studies that have examined the association between polyunsaturated fats and cancer without determining what kind of polyunsaturates were being eaten, or how they were being processed, have produced mixed findings.

FATS THAT HEAL

There is, however, growing evidence that an increased intake of Omega-3 fats (found in flax seeds and fish such as salmon, herring, mackerel and tuna) may reduce the risk of cancer. It is well documented that these fats help reduce inflammation and it is thought to prevent the expression of genes that promote cancer. Also, when the body is in a state of inflammation there is an increased chance of a cancer progressing into the metastatic phase with secondaries developing. Minimising inflammation through the use of Omega-3 fats, reduces the likelihood of this progression.[25] Recent studies have shown that lowering total dietary fats, limiting saturated fats and improving the ratio of Omega-3 to Omega-6 oils is likely to reduce the risk of breast cancer.[26] Omega-3 fats derived from fish oils appear to be most protective.[27] Scientists at Patras

University Medical School in Greece found that after 40 days of taking supplements – 18mg fish oil, 115mg DHA and 200mg vitamin E – malnourished cancer patients had significantly higher T-cell levels and an improved ratio of T-helper to T-suppressor cells, indicating improved immune strength.[28]

The general consensus, both for cancer prevention and overall health, is that we should reduce our intake of saturated fats (principally from meat, dairy products and eggs) and processed or damaged fat (from fried foods and processed foods), and increase our intake of seeds, nuts and their cold-pressed oils or fish. The best seeds are those high in Omega-3 fats, namely flax, followed by pumpkin seeds. These need to be eaten raw and the fats are protected by vitamin E which is naturally present in seeds. An additional supplement of vitamin E may further protect these important essential fats from oxidation.

It is important to use only cold-pressed oils for salad dressings. Cold-pressed olive oil, rich in monounsaturated not polyunsaturated fat, has also been shown to be protective.

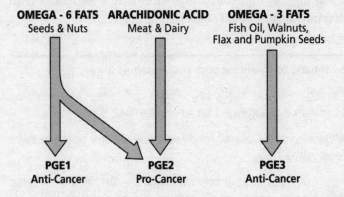

Figure 7 – Good fats and bad fats

Eating fried food, whatever the oil, has been linked to increased risk for a number of cancers.

EAT MORE CARBOHYDRATES

One way to decrease fat intake is to eat more carbohydrates. A study which examined women who ate a diet low in fat and high in carbohydrates over two years found that the women had changes in breast tissue composition that may be linked to a reduced risk of developing breast cancer.[29]

Since carbohydrates also have fewer calories than fat, this is also a great way to cut back on calories. Children whose diets are high in calories are at greater risk of developing cancer in later life. A report in the *British Medical Journal* examined a 1937 study of the diets of nearly 4000 youngsters who were then traced in later life. The researchers found that the children who had had the highest-calorie diets had a 20 per cent higher risk of dying from cancer.[30] An analysis of the diets of colon cancer patients and a control group showed that a high calorie intake was associated with a higher risk of getting the disease.[31] Diets high in complex carbohydrates and low in fat are also high in fibre and a high-fibre diet is associated with protection against colon cancer.[32]

In summary, to maximise your protection from cancer:

■ Eat fish – herring, mackerel, salmon and tuna – and minimise your intake of saturated fat from meat and dairy products.

■ Minimise your intake of fried food. Boil, steam, poach or bake food instead.

■ Add flax seeds to your breakfast and use flax seed oil in salad dressings. Generally avoid refined vegetable oils, using only cold-pressed oils.

CHAPTER 11

THE FIBRE FACTOR

Most people think of fibre as roughage – the indigestible part of plant foods which helps to clean out our insides. What fibre actually does is absorb water in the digestive tract, thereby bulking out faecal matter, which then passes more easily through the body. This means that our exposure to carcinogen-containing foods is shorter. It also minimises the formation of carcinogens which can happen if the food passes through slowly, and, in effect, rots inside us.

Not surprisingly, having enough fibre in your diet correlates with a lower risk of colorectal cancer. There is little doubt that the modern diet – high in alcohol, sugar and fat, and low in fibre – wreaks havoc on the digestive tract. Such a diet disrupts the sensitive balance of beneficial bacteria there, inflames the digestive tract wall and disturbs the gut-associated immune system.

All this is known as 'dysbiosis' and can easily be tested by stool analyses which measure the presence of certain markers of digestive disease. These include butyric acid and beta-glucoronidase. Butyric acid is a kind of fat that actually feeds and nourishes the digestive tract. A certain proportion of fibre is fermented into butyric acid. Without this source of fuel, the digestive tract is more likely to become inflamed, paving the way for colon cancer.[33] Having too much beta-glucoronidase is another useful marker for cancer risk, both of the digestive tract and of the breast. Beta-glucoronidase is a carcinogen made within a digestive tract in a state of dysbiosis. It interferes with the liver's ability to break down oestrogen, which results in its continued circulation, thereby contributing to oestrogen dominance, a known risk factor for breast cancer.

This may explain why a study in China concluded that consumption of foods rich in fibre (as well as vitamin C and carotene) helped protect against breast cancer.[34] In another study from Uruguay an examination of the diets of over 700 women found a strong link between dietary fibre intake and a reduction in the risk of breast cancer in both pre- and post-menopausal women.[35]

The best way to increase your fibre intake is to eat wholefoods, such as wholegrains, lentils, beans, nuts, seeds and vegetables, all of which contain fibre. Some of the fibre in vegetables is destroyed by cooking so you should also eat something raw every day.

CHAPTER 12

COFFEE, TEA AND ALCOHOL – THE WHOLE TRUTH

There is no question that alcohol is a powerful carcinogen. It damages intestinal bacteria and has been reported to convert gut bacteria into secondary metabolites that increase proliferation of cells in the colon, initiating cancer. It can also be absorbed directly into the mucosal cells that line the digestive tract, and converted into aldehyde, which interferes with DNA repair and promotes tumour development. In addition, some alcoholic drinks contain the carcinogen urethrane. According to the World Health Organisation, drinking alcohol has been linked to cancer of the throat, mouth, larynx, pharynx, oesophagus, bladder, breast and liver, with a substantially higher risk for those who smoke too. The Cancer Research Fund adds colorectal cancer to this list and cites hundreds of studies associating alcohol with increased cancer incidence.[36]

One study found a greater risk of breast cancer for those who drink, while the Public Health Department in Japan found alcohol consumption to be a major risk factor for colorectal cancer. Another reported a suppression of the immune system during acute alcohol intoxication as well as an increased risk of cancers 'metastasising' or spreading, due to decreased activity of the natural killer immune cells (which protect against both cancer cells and infections). Whether there is a 'safe' level, below which no risk occurs, is debatable.

HOW MUCH IS TOO MUCH?

The World Cancer Research Fund says that, 'Alcohol consumption is not recommended. If consumed at all, limit alcoholic drinks to less than two drinks a day for men and one for women.' For breast cancer, the risk increases at even one drink a day. For oesophageal and laryngeal cancer, the risk is five to ten times higher at about 120g a day compared to none. (A unit of alcohol – half a pint of beer, a glass of wine or a shot of spirit – provides about 10g alcohol.) One review of six clinical trials, involving a total of 322,000 women, concluded that drinking between 2.8 and 5.6 glasses of wine a day (or the equivalent in beers or spirits) gave a person a 40 per cent higher chance of getting breast cancer.[37] Another study, which followed over 27,000 men for up to eight years in Finland, found that the risk of colorectal cancer increased with the amount of alcohol consumed.[38] Below three drinks a week there is no clear evidence of risk.

If you are going to drink, red wine is probably your best choice. It has been well publicised that substances in red wine have shown a protective effect against cancer and heart disease. As with many foods, it is likely that this is due to its anti-oxidant properties. One study which involved feeding mice a diet including red wine found that those given the wine were free of tumours for 40 per cent longer than those not given wine.[39] You could, of course, eat grapes or drink red grape juice instead and obtain the anti-oxidants from grapes without the alcohol!

Drinking alcohol and smoking is a lethal combination. Both can initiate cancer. Alcohol's suppressive effect on the immune system means it increases the risk of any cancer spreading; hence it is considered a 'co-carcinogen' for cancers of the oesophagus, larynx, lung and stomach.

THE DANGERS OF CAFFEINE

While some studies have shown an increased incidence of pancreatic cancer with coffee consumption,[40] further studies have not shown such an association. Over the last decade considerable research has been done on the cancer–coffee link. Most of these studies have come to the conclusion that coffee is unlikely to increase the risk of any cancer, except possibly for bladder cancer. It is highly unlikely that the consumption of two or three cups of coffee a day adds any cancer risk.

TEA – IS IT GOOD FOR YOU?

Tea, on the other hand, is good or bad depending on which kind you drink and how you drink it. Green tea, now available in healthfood stores, is associated with decreasing risk for stomach cancer. Black tea, which also contains anti-oxidants, may possibly confer protection, not risk. One clinical trial on mice showed that those given black tea had 54 per cent fewer cancers than those given water and significantly fewer than those given green tea.[41]

However, drinking a lot of tea or coffee is not recommended from an overall health point of view. Both contain addictive stimulants, and too many stimulants have negative effects on mental performance, stress and energy levels.

One tea, maté, drunk in large quantities in South America, appears to increase the risk for mouth and oesophageal cancer. However, so too does drinking very hot drinks as this can damage the membrane that lines the throat and oesophagus.

Overall, the general advice is:

- Don't drink alcohol and, if you do, limit your intake to two drinks a day, and ideally three or four drinks a week, preferably choosing red wine.

- Drink green tea and 'red' herb teas, such as rooibosch, rose-hip, hibiscus and berry teas, which are rich in anti-oxidants or regular tea in preference to coffee. However, for general health, don't drink excessive amounts of either.

PART 3

ANTI-CANCER LIFESTYLE FACTORS

CHAPTER 13

PROTECTING YOURSELF FROM RADIATION

There is no question that radiation initiates cancer and that we are all exposed to substantial levels of it. The questions are: what kind and how much radiation significantly affects your risk of developing cancer?

We are all exposed to radiation from the atmosphere, and not just from man-made sources – in fact, two-thirds of our radiation exposure is from nature. There are naturally occurring radioactive materials in air, food and water. We receive the majority of our radiation from natural sources, and the minority from X-rays, nuclear incidents or leaks, and possibly from other factors such as mobile phones.

'Radiation' is a broad term which includes such things as light waves, radio waves and microwaves. However it is most often used to mean ionising radiation – that is, radiation that produces free oxidising radicals, which, in turn, can initiate cancer (see Chapter 2). The long-term consequences of excessive exposure can include leukaemia and other kinds of cancer, as well as infertility, eye cataracts and skin damage.

HOW RADIATION WORKS

Not all radiation, however, is ionising radiation. To understand what does and doesn't put you at risk, it's helpful to understand how radiation works. Atoms, when 'excited', give off energy. This energy travels as a wave that radiates out from the source – hence the term 'radiation'. If the wave has a high frequency it has a lot of energy – it can pass through things and can trigger changes (i.e. generate those harmful 'free radicals'). The radiation that comes off uranium, for example, fits into this category. The sun also emits high-frequency radiation.

However, it isn't just the frequency that determines how potentially harmful the radiation is. It's also the intensity – that is the power of the signal. So, although the sun emits high-frequency radiation, by the time it gets to us across millions of miles of space, especially if passing through layers of clouds, it's relatively harmless. Not so, however, if you spend an hour in the scorching heat at the Equator. So the higher the frequency, the stronger the signal, and the closer you are to the source – the more high-energy particles you are exposed to, with an accompanying increase in the generation of harmful free radicals. On the other hand, a low-frequency signal, like a radio wave, may generate a bit of heat but doesn't contain anything like enough energy to generate free radicals and harm you.

THE DANGERS OF COMPUTERS AND TV

The radiation that comes off your radio, TV and computer screen is not likely to present any health risk because it is low-energy, although it's a good idea to have some ventilation, as many appliances dry the air and generate heat. Watching TV a foot away from the screen 24 hours a day might, however, pose a health hazard. Some people choose to fit filters on their computer screens to cut down the radiation. Generally, it is a good idea to sit as far away from the screen as you realistically can so that the energy in the particles dissipates before it gets to you.

Microwave ovens are high-energy, but the waves are contained within a metal box so you are not exposed.

However, the intense heat generated by microwaving fatty foods generates free radicals, much like frying, so this is not recommended.

MOBILE PHONES – ARE THEY A HEALTH HAZARD?

The frequency of the signal from a mobile phone is quite low. However, the strength of the signal and, most importantly, the fact that the source (the phone) is right next to your brain, has raised concerns about whether the energy is strong enough to generate free radicals and hence increase cancer risk.

New Australian research has found a doubling of tumours in mice exposed to radiation at mobile phone frequencies. In research led by Dr Michael Repacholi, who heads the WHO programme studying the possible hazards of electromagnetic fields, the mice were exposed to pulsed radiation for one hour a day for nine to 18 months. At the end of the trial, the mice showed twice as many B–cell lymphomas.[1] (B–cell effects are implicated in roughly 85 per cent of all cancers.) Additional research by Lester Packer and colleagues also links electro-magnetic fields to increases in cancer.[2]

Although mice are not men this finding is worrying because there is evidence of an increase in the incidence of brain cancer in correlation with the widespread use of mobile phones. Dr Andrew Davidson, at the Fremantle Hospital in Australia, analysed the incidence of brain cancer in Australia from 1982 to 1992. His survey shows double the number of cases.[3] Brain cancer is also on the increase in Britain and the US for no apparent reason.

The World Health Organisation has already called for more international research to find out whether there really is a risk from frequent use of mobile phones.[4] Until we know the answer, it would seem prudent to use them infrequently or use them with earphones.

X-RAYS

Another definite source of high-energy radiation is X-rays. For this reason it is not advisable to have them frequently. This, of course, raises a dilemma when it comes to mammograms, introduced as an early warning system for identifying breast cancer. Some argue that, if these were used as a regular screening programme, the cumulative effects of the X-rays might counteract the small benefit achieved in early diagnosis.

While the general recommendation is to have three-yearly screens, Dr Karol Sikora, Professor of Oncology at Hammersmith Hospital, believes that, under the age of 50, there is no benefit from screening and he doesn't recommend it. It is certainly not something a pregnant woman would be advised to do. Dr John Lee says that mammograms often pick up microcalcifications (small calcium deposits) in the breast. Whether or not these warrant treatment is a matter of debate, since microcalcifications may not be cancer as we know it. Both Sikora and Lee favour regular breast examination to identify any suspect changes.

Ironically, another major source of radiation exposure is radiotherapy, used to treat cancer. This is only recommended when there is an advanced malignant tumour that can be pinpointed to minimise surrounding damage. The radiation damages the DNA of the cancer cells and obviously damages some healthy cells too. Radiation treatment is carcinogenic in itself, and as such, requires more serious consideration for cancer treatment.

NUCLEAR POWER – IS IT SAFE?

Despite denials by the nuclear industry, there is some evidence to show an increased incidence of childhood leukaemia in certain regions adjacent to nuclear power generators. For example, research published in the *British Medical Journal* in October 1987 looked at two groups of children – 1068 born near Sellafield and 1564 born outside the area but attending nearby schools.[5] The leukaemia and cancer cases occurred only in those children born near the Sellafield nuclear reprocessing plant. And there are other areas of 'leukaemia clusters' adjacent to nuclear installations. However, it is also true that major improvements have been made in safety standards and it is quite possible that such risk is confined to old reactors and errors, such as leaks. However, there are good grounds for society to remain extra-vigilant about the safety measures surrounding the handling of nuclear fuel.

NATURAL RADIATION

Apart from the effects of sunlight (discussed in the next chapter), the largest 'natural' source of radiation is radon. Radon is a naturally occurring gas that is present in some areas due to the underlying geology. As uranium in rocks decays, it produces radon, which escapes – colourless and odourless – into the air. Uranium and its decay product radium are found naturally in rocks and soil and also in building materials such as wood, bricks and concrete. When the decay byproducts are inhaled (contained in small dust particles), the radioactive molecules settle in the lungs and irradiate intensely at close range for many years.

In the open air any radon is mixed and diluted with air and quickly dispersed. Inside buildings, however, it is released from construction materials and from the ground, and is then inhaled by the occupants.

Recent surveys carried out in the UK suggest that residents in some parts of the country are at greater risk than others. The South-West seems to be the most affected area but there are other local 'hot spots'. Areas with high granite are the most affected. In some cases the radiation dose from radon accounts for over 50 per cent of the total natural radiation. At this level, it could be responsible for several hundred deaths from cancer per year. A study by the Imperial Cancer Research Fund shows that people exposed to radon have a 20 per cent higher chance of contracting lung cancer; indeed it attributes 1800 lung cancer deaths a year to radon exposure.[6]

If you live in a high granite area, most common in the South-West of England, contact your local Environmental Health Officer to find out what your radon exposure is likely to be. When radon levels are high, it is better to use certain building materials than others. Adequate ventilation under floorboards is also important to remove the radioactive compounds before they can build up to significant levels.

PROTECTING YOURSELF FROM RADIATION

Radioactive elements can be taken up by the body and incorporated into your tissues where they continue to emit radiation. An example is radioactive iodine, which is taken up by the thyroid gland. By ensuring a more than adequate intake of minerals (in this case iodine), tissues are saturated with non-radioactive elements and are therefore protected.

However, the more forms of radiation (for example, from the sun or mobile phones) may generate free radicals (oxidants) that can harm body cells. So, in addition to minimising exposure, the most important protection factor is to ensure an optimal intake of anti-oxidant nutrients, such as vitamins A, C and E and the minerals zinc and selenium. These help protect against the damage caused by ionising radiation.

In summary:

■ Only have an X-ray if it is absolutely essential.

- If you use a mobile phone, use it infrequently and use an ear-phone attachment.

- If you suspect you live in a high radon area, check with your local Environmental Health Office and make sure your house is well ventilated.

- Take anti-oxidant supplements daily (see Chapter 24).

CHAPTER 14

DYING FOR A TAN?

The link between skin cancer incidence and sun exposure is far more tenuous than we have been led to believe. Did you know, for example, that the closer you get to the Equator, the lower the incidence of cancer? Sunlight, it appears, is both good for us and bad for us. On the one hand, there is evidence that light-skinned people exposed to strong sunlight have more skin cancer. On the other hand, there is some evidence that people deprived of natural sunlight, spending hours in artificial lighting, may actually have a higher cancer incidence.

Natural sunlight does generally boost immunity and improve health. (For a fuller discussion of the health effects of light, read *Daylight Robbery* by Dr Damien Downing – see Recommended Reading.) One major reason for this could be that exposure to sunlight stimulates vitamin D synthesis in the skin. Although the mechanism by which this may happen is not yet clearly understood, vitamin D has been shown to slow down the proliferation of some cancer cells.[7] This is consistent with evidence that patients with advanced breast cancer who have high vitamin D levels have a better chance of survival. It may also explain why breast cancer rates are lower in sunnier parts of the world. Interestingly, natural sunlight actually stimulates cell growth but not during exposure or the first hour thereafter.[8] So we have an hour's grace to mop up oxidants and repair any DNA damage in readiness for the burst of increased cellular activity following exposure to sunlight.

However, there is a limit to the benefits of sunshine, especially if you are fair-skinned. People with fair skin (low in melanin), who burn easily and rarely tan when they sunbathe, do have a higher risk of skin cancer when exposed to the high-energy UV radiation of the sun. As research proceeds, it is becoming more and more evident that it is the combination of a certain skin type with excessive sun exposure that increases risk of cancer. Other research has, however, shown that genetic factors (such as the number of moles a person has, or their natural skin colour) can be more important in determining cancer risk than the amount of time they spend exposed to the sun.

Most skin cancer, although quite common, is easily treated and rarely fatal. However, about 2 per cent of all skin cancers are of a more insidious nature and are likely to metastasise quickly, spreading to other parts of the body. These are melanomas. If anything, the evidence is tending to show that inherited characteristics, rather than just sun exposure, may play a greater part in the incidence of melanoma. Some experts also think that one big, blistery burn as a child can also increase risk as an adult, perhaps by damaging the skin's immune cells. Since 1935 the risk of developing melanoma has increased twenty-fold. Dr Marianne Berwick, of the Sloan-Kettering Cancer Center in New York, found that those with a large number of moles, or with red or blond hair and lighter-coloured eyes or with pale skin, had a six times higher risk. However, the rapid increase in melanoma does suggest that factors other than genetics are involved – greater UV exposure due to changes in holiday habits and ozone layer depletion are two possible candidates. Over the past decade there has been a 7 per cent increase in UV exposure in Europe.

The combination of fair skin, excessive exposure to strong

sunlight and alcohol or smoking is definitely bad news. During strong sunlight exposure, the risk of oxidant damage to the skin (i.e. burning) is at its highest. Smoking introduces oxidants into the lungs and bloodstream. Alcohol, meanwhile, suppresses the immune system, weakening the body's natural defences. This is also not a good time to be eating a lot of fried food.

If you are lying on a sunny beach it is therefore best to use a sunscreen that also contains anti-oxidants. Also, eat plenty of anti-oxidant-rich foods, such as fresh fruit and vegetables. These high anti-oxidant foods are exactly those found in parts of the world where the sun shines long and strong. So nature protects you if you eat local foods.

Sunscreens do their job by absorbing UV energy before it gets through to our skin. There are two kinds of UV rays: UVA, excess of which depresses the immune system and is more associated with ageing and less with cancer; UVB which causes sunburn and damage to skin cells and can initiate cancer. Ideally, you want to limit exposure to both since UVA can weaken immune responses vital for dealing with damaged cells.

But not all sunscreens are equally effective. Research has shown that chemicals found in some sun creams may actually pass on excess energy from the sun's rays into the skin, where it damages DNA. These chemicals are Padimate-O, PABA-O or Escalol 507, says Dr John Knowland from Oxford University. The research was done in test tubes, so it has yet to be discovered whether the same effect takes place in humans.[9]

Octylmethoxycinnamate, octylsalicylate, tea salicylate and homosalate all effectively absorb the dangerous portions of UVB light. Titanium dioxide and zinc oxide also absorb part of the UVA spectrum and scatter or reflect the sun's rays. These two are often employed in higher SPF (sun protection factor) blocks. The SPF number indicates how long you can stay in the sun without burning e.g. SPF2 means twice as long because these blocks absorb 50 per cent of the energy hitting the skin. Better sunscreens also contain anti-oxidants which protect the skin by mopping up oxidants as well as improving immune defences.

The Australian motto is 'slip, slap, slop' – slip on a shirt, slap on a hat, and slop on some sunscreen, especially if you're fair skinned. Melanomas start from moles so it's a good idea to check for any changes in moles, especially on the feet, genital folds, breasts, armpits and scalp. If detected early the success rate is good. However, if melanomas go undetected for six months this type of cancer is often fatal.

In summary, based on the evidence to date, you should:

- Minimise the amount of time you spend in strong sunlight, especially if you have fair skin, light coloured eyes and lots of moles.

- Use a good sunscreen that contains antioxidants, not lower than SPF 7.

- Eat plenty of anti-oxidant-rich foods – especially fruits and vegetables.

- Take an anti-oxidant supplement.

CHAPTER 15

PESTICIDES AND PLASTICS

Possibly one of the most underestimated contributors to the epidemic of cancer is the combined effect of humanity's exposure to man-made chemicals. However, this statement must be qualified for two reasons. Firstly, we know remarkably little about most of the thousands of chemicals to which we are all unwittingly exposed and virtually nothing about their effects in combination. Secondly, some of the cancer research organisations are very closely linked to, and funded by, the medical/industrial chemical industry who can influence the direction of their research; consequently, little research is being done into the effects of such chemicals. However, the investigations that have been done raise some serious questions about certain pesticides and chemicals, particularly those used in the plastics industry.

PROBLEM PESTICIDES

Currently, the three areas of most concern in relation to pesticides are their links with breast cancer, childhood cancers and increased cancer incidence among farmers.

Each year in the UK 16,000 women die of breast cancer. The particularly high incidence in Lincolnshire compared to average – where there are many farms – may be partly explained by the high use of pesticides on certain crops. A study by Greenpeace and several women's groups looked at the possible links between various environmental pollutants and breast cancer.[10] They found that women have up to ten times the normal risk of getting cancer when they are shown to have high levels of pesticides and other toxic chemicals in their body. The groups specifically looked at dioxin, PCB, and DDT. These chlorine-based chemicals – organochlorines – are commonly found in fish and waterfowl and can end up in many women's diets. The researchers say that when similar chemicals were banned in Israel, breast cancer rates dropped sharply.

Many organochlorines do not degrade easily and remain in the environment for a long time, which means they can easily enter the food chains of wildlife and humans. Lindane is the one remaining organochlorine which is still widely used for agricultural purposes in Britain. It is also used in medicine, veterinary products and to treat timber for pest control. The use of Lindane in arable farming in 1992–3 was more than double that of 1987–8. One-third of all Lindane used in 1992 involved the treatment of sugar beet. Over 70 per cent of this crop is grown in eastern counties such as Lincolnshire.

Although Lindane breaks down more easily than other organochlorine pesticides, scientists have reported that it breaks down into even more dangerous substances which may be cancer-forming. Dr Leon Bradlow, of the Strang-Cornell Cancer Research Laboratory, New York, has found that Lindane stimulates the production of a hormone capable of damaging DNA and causes cancerous changes in breast cells in the test tube. Lindane has been detected in cow's milk and dairy products worldwide and it is probable that traces of Lindane have been present at low levels in UK milk for decades. Sugar beet is a major component of cattle feed and it is suggested that this may be the route into the cow and finally to the milk. Researchers tested one bag of sugar beet pellets at random and found a trace of Lindane – despite published reports claiming that Lindane has never been found in a sugar beet ingredient in animal feed.[11]

PESTICIDES, CHILDREN AND CANCER

Research from New Zealand has clearly shown that pesticide levels are highest in children, especially young children.[12] This is probably because they consume more food in relation to their body mass than adults and generally consume more fruit, which is heavily sprayed. The New Zealand survey found that intake of organophosphate pesticides was twice as high in young children, aged one to three, than in male adults. This finding is particularly worrying because the introduction of either carcinogens or hormone-disrupting chemicals while a child is still developing has greater implications for their future health. Animal studies have certainly shown that young animals are much more susceptible to the effects of a wide range of pesticides in use today.

Studies looking at the association between lifestyle factors and childhood cancer have frequently identified chemical exposure as an associated risk factor. A study of 84 children in Maryland, USA, who had developed brain cancer, versus those who hadn't, found that those with brain cancer were more likely to have been exposed to insecticides in the home.[13] The US Children's Cancer Study Group found an increased risk of leukemia in 204 children whose parents used pesticides in their home and garden,[14] a finding reported by other researchers.[15]

One source of organophosphates to which some children are exposed is anti-headlice lotions. With some manufacturers suggesting that children leave these in the hair overnight, it seems that there is reasonable cause for concern. Natural alternatives include suffocating the lice by soaking the hair with olive oil and covering it with a showercap; the lice can then be combed out. Another method is to add tea tree oil to the children's shampoo and leave it on for 10 minutes.

Another indication that exposure to agrochemicals is of real concern comes from statistics on the incidence of cancer among farmers. Generally speaking, farmers are healthier than the average person. Yet there is a disproportionate increase in the incidence of several cancers, including leukaemia, non-Hodgkin's lymphoma and cancers of the brain and prostate. In the US the amount of pesticides sprayed annually has gone from 50 million pounds in the 1940s to one billion pounds in the 1980s. The average person now has up to a gallon of pesticides and herbicides sprayed on the fruit and vegetables they eat each year.

These agrochemicals are designed to kill and there is no doubt that human exposure is undesirable. While a number of pesticides, herbicides and fungicides are known to act as carcinogens, it is very hard to prove which ones are a problem, at which doses, and also what their combined effects are. Broadly speaking, there is plenty of evidence that eating fruit and vegetables reduces risk, but perhaps the benefit would be even greater if the fruits and vegetables were organic.

Even though the research hasn't yet been done, there is certainly a logical case for choosing organically grown foods on the basis that these chemicals are 'guilty until proven innocent'.

PLASTIC DANGERS

Perhaps even more worrying is the discovery that a number of chemicals used in plastics are also potentially carcinogenic. These include alkylphenols such as nonylphenol and octylphenol, biphenolic compounds such as bisphenol A, and phthalates. These chemicals are used in domestic detergents and toiletries, so the chances are that you have some of them in your bathroom. If they had to be listed on food packaging, you'd probably find them in your kitchen too. They are often used to coat metal containers such as food cans, and they can also be in soft plastic liners in juice cartons, film wrapping and other plastic wrappers. The trouble is they don't have to be declared. So, until they are banned or legislation is passed requiring declaration of such chemicals, there's really no way of knowing.

The problem with this group of chemicals is that they can disrupt hormone signals – they generally have an oestrogenic effect (see Chapter 3). It is this effect that is associated with the increasing risk of hormone-related cancers. Fuelled by concerns about rising cancer incidence and falling sperm counts, many environmental groups are campaigning for the disclosure, if not the banning, of such hormone-disrupting chemicals. Included in this list are chlorine compounds such as organochlorines, polychlorinated biphenyls (PCBs) and dioxins. These are used in farming, in paper production, and in industrial processes. Even though PCBs and DDT (an organochlorine) have been banned, they are non-biodegradable which means that significant levels can still be detected in each of us. Also on the suspect list is the food additive butylated hydroxyanisole (BHA).

According to Dr Theo Colborn, co-author of the book *Our Stolen Future* (see Recommended Reading), there are now 100,000 synthetic chemicals on the world market, including 15,000 synthetic chlorinated compounds – a category of chemicals that has come under attack because of their persistence in the environment and record of causing health problems. The US exports 40 million pounds of compounds known to be endocrine-disrupters each year and anyone willing to spend the money on tests will find at least 250 contaminants in his or her body fat.

For example, in six months of breast-feeding, a baby in Europe receives the maximum recommended lifetime dose of dioxin.[16] In Spain, an analysis of 20 brands of food in cans which are now lined with plastic (as are many drinks cartons) showed that most contained significant levels of bisphenol-A, some at a level 27 times higher than that known to cause the proliferation of breast cancer cells. These are a few of the disturbing statements in this book which links such chemicals to endocrine-related diseases including breast cancer, endometriosis, prostate problems – and the decline in male fertility.

Once again, until more research is carried out, it is impossible to quantify the real dangers of exposure to these chemicals. While it is impossible to avoid them all, there are many changes you can make to your diet and lifestyle that are likely to substantially decrease your exposure to such hormone-disrupting and potentially carcinogenic chemicals. These are as follows:

- **Eat organic.** This instantly minimises your exposure to pesticides and herbicides. When you are eating non-organic produce wash it in an acidic medium, made by adding 1 tablespoon vinegar to a bowl of water. This will reduce some, but not all pesticides.

- **Filter all drinking water.** I recommend getting a water filter that you install under the sink, made from stainless steel (not plastic or aluminium), employing some kind of carbon-filtration system. While not proven to remove all hormone-disrupting chemicals, this should decrease your load. The alternative is spring water, bottled in glass.

- **Reduce your intake of fatty foods.** Non-biodegradable chemicals accumulate in the food chain in animal fat. Minimising your intake of animal fat – meat and dairy produce – lessens your exposure. There is no need to limit essential fats in nuts and seeds.

- **Never heat food in plastic.*** This means saying goodbye to microwaved TV dinners. If you have to have them, transfer the food into a glass container before heating.

- **Minimise fatty foods exposed to flexible plastics.**★ Some chemicals that keep plastics flexible easily pass out of the plastic into fatty food such as crisps, cheese, butter, chocolate, pies, etc.

- **Minimise liquid foods exposed to flexible plastics.**★ This not only includes fruit juices in cardboard packs, which have a plastic inner lining, but also some fruits and vegetables in cans, which may again have a plastic inner lining.

- **Minimise exposure of food to flexible plastics.**★ This means using paper bags whenever possible as opposed to buying everything in plastic trays, covered with clingfilm.

- **Switch to natural detergents.** Use only ecological detergent products for washing up, washing clothes and body washing, made by companies who declare all their ingredients. And check that the ingredients exclude the suspect chemicals listed on pp. 100–1. Also, rinse dishes and cutlery after washing up.

- **Don't use pesticides in your garden.** Some pesticides are hormone-disrupters. Unless you're sure yours isn't, it is better not to spray. The incidence of childhood cancer is higher in homes where the gardens are sprayed with pesticides.

★It is currently impossible for you to know whether the plastics you use contain hormone-disrupting chemicals or not.

CHAPTER 16

ACTIVE AND PASSIVE SMOKING

The association between smoking and cancer is, without question, the major reason why lung cancer is now the most common cause of cancer deaths in the world. Incidence from country to country correlates very closely with number of cigarettes smoked, except in certain parts of the world. For example, in Japan and in rural China there is a weaker correlation between number of cigarettes and incidence of lung cancer. There is therefore a very real possibility that at least two other factors need to be taken into account: diet and exposure to exhaust fumes or industrial pollution.

Few people realise how important our intake of anti-oxidant nutrients is in protecting us against the harmful effects of smoking. A study of 265,000 people in Japan found that those with a low intake of beta-carotene (the form of vitamin A found in fruits and vegetables) had a higher risk of lung cancer.[17] Furthermore, a study of employees of Western Electric, published in *The Lancet* medical journal, found that beta-carotene status was as significant as smoking in determining risk of lung cancer.[18] In this study they found that 6.5 per cent of heavy smokers with a low beta-carotene status developed cancer. This percentage dropped to 0.8 per cent for heavy smokers with a high beta-carotene status. Conversely, non-smokers with a low beta-carotene status also had an 0.8 per cent risk, while non-smokers with a high beta-carotene status had no risk at all.

This demonstrates that smoking and diet play equally important roles in protecting against lung cancer. Smoking also increases the risk of other kinds of cancer, including other parts of the airways, pancreas, cervix and bladder[19] and diet offers protection against these forms of cancer too.

While it is known that the number of years a person smokes, the number of cigarettes they smoke, and the tar content all increase risk, research shows that another highly critical factor is the age at which a person starts smoking. The risk of death from lung cancer is almost double for those who start smoking before the age of 15, compared to those who start in their twenties.[20] This underlines the importance of campaigns dissuading teenagers from taking up the habit.

OTHER CAUSES OF LUNG CANCER

However, there are undoubtedly other risk factors involved in lung cancer that have been downplayed in the rush to point the finger at smoking alone. The importance of considering such factors is evident when you look at some surprising facts: the incidence of lung cancer in non-smokers has doubled over recent decades; the incidence of adenocarcinoma of the lung (which is less clearly related to smoking) has also continued to increase; and in the US the incidence is much higher in black men than in white. Professor Samuel Epstein believes that occupational exposure to carcinogens used in a wide variety of industries, and exposure to industrial pollutants and exhaust fumes, particularly from diesel, play an important part in non-smoking-related lung cancer.[21]

PASSIVE SMOKING

For non-smokers the key issue is to what extent other people's smoke contributes to their cancer risk. A number of studies have been conducted over the past decade, many of which have shown a slightly higher risk for lung cancer, and, in women, for breast cancer, when exposed to other people's smoke. One such study looked at deaths form lung cancer in women living in Pennsylvania.[22] Women who neither smoked nor were exposed to smoke had a quarter of the incidence of death from lung cancer of women exposed to other people's smoke. The incidence of death from lung cancer among smokers was approximately ten times that of passive smokers. Other studies confirm this trend, though more research is needed. One analysis of studies to date concludes that 'the relative risk [of a passive smoker contracting lung cancer] is about two-fold higher [than an non-exposed, non-smoker.'[23] There is also some evidence that women who are exposed to other people's cigarette smoke have an increased risk of breast cancer.[24]

Despite the general decline in smoking in the Western world a staggering number of people do smoke. In the US 487 billion cigarettes are smoked annually. In the UK the figure is 83 billion. There is a long way to go before this major contributor to cancer risk is eliminated.

CHAPTER 17

....

THE ART OF CHEMICAL SELF-DEFENCE

Many common substances to which we are exposed are known carcinogens. Some of these, but by no means all, have been discussed in earlier chapters. Although the levels that trigger cancer may be a lot higher than most people are normally exposed to, a cursory look down the checklist below will show that, like most people, you are probably exposed to a large number of potential carcinogens. You may wonder what the cumulative effect is of such exposure to a number of known carcinogens, albeit at low doses. In truth, no one knows, but the results from the laboratory of Professor Ana Soto and Professor Carlos Sonnenschein at Boston's Tufts University are alarming. They were investigating the levels at which known hormone-disrupting chemicals would cause proliferation of breast cancer cells. They then exposed these cells to combinations of five or ten chemicals, each at a tenth of the dose that would produce proliferation. Sure enough, there was a cocktail effect such that, in combination, these chemicals were ten times as powerful, producing rapid proliferation of breast cancer cells.[25]

HOW TO DECREASE YOUR EXPOSURE TO KNOWN CARCINOGENS

The following factors are carcinogenic only at certain concentrations. While it is ideal to minimise your overall exposure or intake, the presence of these in small amounts may not constitute a risk. After all, it is now impossible to avoid all carcinogens, no matter where or how you live.

General

- Tobacco smoke, whether or not you are a smoker.

- Coal tar and petrochemical derivatives used in some hair oils, lipsticks and cosmetics, perfumes, soaps, deodorants and anti-perspirants.

- Plastics containing vinyl chloride, polystyrene, and certain plasticisers (e.g. phthalates), used in food containers, kitchen utensils, clothes, furniture, curtains, bedding, etc.

- Fluoride in water supplies and in toothpaste.

- Epoxy resins, glues, etc.

- Carbon tetrachloride (used in cleaning fluids, etc.).

- Industrial detergents containing alkylphenols.

- Many factory emissions, e.g. iron and steel founding, rubber industry and especially those containing sulphuric acid.

- Car, lorry, bus and boat exhausts, and fumes from central heating boilers (oil, coal or gas-fired).

- Working daily in boot and shoe manufacture and repair, furniture manufacture, painting, etc.

- Dioxins produced by incineration of chlorine-containing chemicals and some processes such as the production of chlorinated hydrocarbons and paper.

- PCBs (polychlorinated biphenyls), although now banned in Europe, are very persistent; they used to be used in ink, paint, plasticisers, capacitators and electricity transformers.

- Brominated flame retardants (BFRs), chemicals added to many products (such as carpets and computers) to reduce fire risk.

- Fluorocarbons, used in many products, from refrigerants and anaesthetics to pesticides and industrial surfactants.

What you can do

- Don't smoke and avoid spending much time around people who do.

- Choose your cosmetics carefully. Most healthfood shops stock less chemical-laden alternatives.

- Use glass, paper and wooden containers and utensils as much as possible in the kitchen.

- Minimise the amount of food you eat that is covered in plastic, especially fatty food such as cheese.

- Use 'environmentally friendlier' detergents.

- If your job involves particularly high exposure to chemicals, wear a mask and gloves and make sure your workplace is well ventilated.

Food and drink

- Chlorine in tap water.

- Pesticides and their residues (see Agricultural chemicals, below).

- Smoked meats and fish (such food often contains creosote and formaldehyde).

- Food preservatives, especially nitrates in bacon, processed meats, non-organic fruit and vegetables, and water (from over-use of nitrogen fertilisers in agriculture).

- Coffee – suspect because roasting produces matrol.

- Decaffeinated coffee contains matrol and other solvents.

- Saccharin and cyclamates (chemical sweeteners).

- Saturated fat (found in dairy produce, meat and meat products, pastry, cakes and puddings, cheese, milk, eggs, fish and chips, and other fried foods).

- Fats heated to high temperatures (above 200°C or 392°F in preparing food).

- Alcohol – risk is significant above one drink a day for women and two drinks a day for men.

- Parsley, celery and parsnips – these and other members of the Umbelliferae family contain carcinogenic psoralens.

- Burnt (charred or dark brown) foods (e.g. toast, cakes, bread).

- Barbecued, charred meat and fish – produces heterocyclic aromatic amines.

- Bleaches (for white bread, etc.).

- Moulds on foodstuffs (such as *Aspergillus flavus*, the toxin aflatoxin and other mycotoxins found in certain moulds), e.g. on nuts, cheese, milk, jam, bread.

- Some anti-oxidant preservatives such as butylated hydroxyanisole (BHA).

What you can do
- Get a good water filter or drink spring water.

- Eat and drink organic produce whenever possible.

- Wash non-organic produce in acidic water – add 1 tablespoon of vinegar to a bowl of water.

- Minimise your consumption of saturated fats (meat and

dairy products), processed meats and smoked foods – choose fish and soya products instead.

- Avoid fried food.

- Eat grilled or barbecued meat and fish infrequently – poach, bake or boil it instead.

- Have no more than one alcoholic drink a day – have an alcohol-free week every now and then.

- Avoid all processed, refined food, especially foods which are high in preservatives and other additives.

- If you drink coffee, go for the organic varieties. Choose water-processed decaffeinated coffee.

- Don't eat food that's starting to go mouldy.

Medical carcinogens

- Chloroform.

- Liquid paraffin.

- X-rays (including radioactive dyes and radio isotopes).

- Mineral oils.

- All coal-derivative products.

- Hormone therapy (contraceptive pills and HRT).

- Certain antibiotics and sulphonamide drugs are strongly suspect.

- Psoralens (used for treating skin complaints).

- Tamoxifen, the anti-cancer drug.

- Dental lacquers that contain bisphenol A.

- Analgesics containing phenacetin.

What you can do

- Only have X-rays when you absolutely have to.

- Use natural alternatives to artificial hormone therapy.

- Use natural alternatives to drugs whenever possible.

Agricultural chemicals

- Atrazine, the commonest pesticide found in UK drinking water.

- Captan, a fungicide.

- Chlorothalonil, a fungicide.

- Chlorpyrifos, an organophosphate.

- DDE, a very persistent breakdown product of DDT.

- Dichlorvos, an organophosphate.

- Dithiocarbamates or EBDCs, fungicides including mancozeb, metiram, thiram and zineb which break down to form ethylene thiourea (ETU).

- Endosulfan, an organochlorine.

- Fenitrothion, an organophosphate.

- Iprodione, a fungicide.

- Malathion, an organophosphate, used in several headlice lotions.

- Permethrin.

- Pirimphos Methyl, an organophosphate.

- Procymidone, a fungicide.

- Vinclozolin, a fungicide.

What you can do

- Choose organic produce whenever possible.

- Don't use any products in your garden or pot plants that contain these chemicals.

- Choose natural alternatives.

Others

- Background nuclear radiation polluting atmosphere, crops, meat and water.

- Certain viruses.

- Radiation from TV sets, computers and mobile phones.

- Radiation from the sun.

What you can do

- Avoid being out in strong sunlight. If you are, cover up or use a good sunscreen, above factor 7.

- If you use a mobile telephone, use an earphone.

For many factors, e.g. smoking, the necessary action is clear-cut: don't smoke. The same can be said for pesticides – eat organic. However, with other factors, there is a limit to how much action we can reasonably take. Because we do not fully understand the effect of combinations of mild carcinogens and because it would take decades to find out, the only sensible way forward is to develop a diet and lifestyle that reduces exposure to as many as possible. Admittedly, all this is easier said than done. But, as long as you are doing all you can to *minimise* your exposure, it's not worth becoming completely obsessive. After all, stress and worry are not helpful either, as you will find out in the next chapter.

CHAPTER 18

....

THE STRESS CONNECTION

Stress and negative emotions play a very important role in the cancer equation. It is well known that cancer is frequently diagnosed in people who have been through a major loss or traumatic event one or two years previously. Cancers normally appear to have a long 'incubation' – usually manifesting ten to 40 years after initial exposure to a carcinogen as in the case of exposure to cigarette smoke and asbestos. Yet, in the case of stress or loss, the time-frame is much quicker.

From what we know about the effects of stress and loss on the immune system, it is highly likely that, in people who succumb to cancer, the process had already begun before the event. The stress then dramatically weakens the immune system, allowing the process to speed up rapidly.

Stress encourages the production and circulation of adrenal hormones. These, in turn, inhibit the immune response by lowering levels of the important white cells. Depression, stress, anxiety, hostility and fatigue all result in poorer function of the immune T-cells.[26] Researchers at Ohio State University College of Medicine and Comprehensive Cancer Center have reported impaired DNA repair in highly distressed people who have difficulty coping with problems.[27]

Stress also dramatically suppresses immune defences in the digestive tract, which is a major entry route for carcinogens into the body. Since about three-quarters of all our immune cells are situated in the digestive tract, this is highly significant. Our first line of defence is a substance called secretory immunoglobulin A (sIgA). Prolonged stress lowers our levels of sIgA, and thus leaves us more vulnerable to the effects of carcinogens in the digestive tract. This may explain why the risk of colorectal cancer becomes greater after a period of high stress.

According to Dr Bernie Siegel's book *Love, Medicine and Miracles* (see Recommended Reading), certain personality types are more prone to cancer. He says the disease is more prevalent in people who do not easily form close bonds or love relationships; also in people who internalise or deny their feelings and do not easily express negative emotions such as anger or frustration. People who are active, assertive, avoid overly nice behavior and have an underlying high sense of self-esteem are less likely to experience unresolved loss, a sense of helplessness or hopeleasness which can weaken the immune system.

Among people who make remarkable recoveries from cancer, there are often reports of having made transformations on many fronts – nutritional, psychological and spiritual. The will to live is indeed a very powerful part of this equation. And meditation and visualisation techniques have been shown to help. Perhaps best documented is the work of Carl and Stephanie Simonton who have demonstrated the power of visualisation techniques in the healing process. These are described in their book *Getting Well Again* (see Recommended Reading). People faced with a potentially life-threatening diagnosis often go through a stage of denial, followed by anger, fuelled by fear. In working through these issues and emotions, a person may come to accept the reality of their situation and, from that position, they will be better equipped to direct their will towards healing.

There are several organisations that support people with cancer through the whole process of dealing with such issues (see Useful Addresses). These groups can provide more information on treatments, including psychological approaches, which will enable you to weigh up the pros and cons and decide whether to use any of the techniques yourself.

PART 4

ANTI-CANCER NUTRIENTS

CHAPTER 19

....

EXPLODING THE MYTHS

Cancer is complex. In most cases it is due to many factors, including exposure to carcinogens that promote cell changes and a poorly functioning immune system. Indeed, these unfavourable circumstances may need to be present for several decades to fuel the process from initiation to diagnosis.

The evidence already shows that we can achieve much greater success in the battle against cancer, not by aggressively treating the disease once it has developed, but by minimising carcinogen exposure and boosting the immune system in the first place. The next three chapters explain this evidence and the importance of optimising your intake of anti-cancer nutrients such as vitamin C, beta-carotene and others. Indeed, it is eating foods high in these nutrients that is associated with a reduced incidence of cancer. The evidence for their critical role is already substantial, yet – strangely – the supplementation of such nutrients is often reported negatively by the media.

BETA-CAROTENE MYTHS

There are over 200 studies showing a beneficial role for beta-carotene in preventing cancer, yet it is isolated reports to the contrary that tend to receive the most media attention. Such was the case when the *Daily Mail* ran an article headlined 'Cancer Alert in Vitamin Pill Probe', telling a story of 28 per cent more cases of lung cancer among a group of smokers supplementing 30mg of vitamin A and 25,000iu of beta-carotene.[1] Confusing, isn't it?

Perhaps that's the intention. A closer look at the figures shows that this 'trend' (which was not statistically significant) actually amounted to the difference between five cases of cancer in 1000 people and six in 1000; these were people who had smoked for years and quite possibly had undetected cancer before starting the trial. Hidden in the figures was another insignificant, and unreported finding. Those who stopped smoking during the trial and took beta-carotene had 20 per cent fewer cases of lung cancer. Does this mean that beta-carotene gives smokers cancer, but protects those who quit? Or that both results are, as the statistics state, a matter of chance, a minor variable, and that a little pill of synthetic beta-carotene (missing all the other anti-oxidants found in natural source beta-carotene) cannot impact on a lifetime of smoking. We may never know: at a cost of £27 million the trial was abandoned.

VITAMIN C MYTHS

Another popular myth is that vitamin C can promote cancer. This has never been demonstrated, but its highly protective effect has. First shown to be a powerful anti-cancer agent in 1971, it wasn't until 20 years later that vitamin C started to be accepted by the medical profession. In 1992, Dr Gladys Block, formerly with the National Cancer Institute, wrote:

I have reviewed the epidemiologic literature, about 140 studies, on the relationship between antioxidant micro-nutrients or their food sources and cancer risk. The data are overwhelmingly consistent. With possibly fewer

than five exceptions, every single study is in the protective direction, and something like 110 to 120 studies
found statistically significant reduced risk with high
intake.

Vitamin C-rich diets reduce the risk of cancer, and high
intakes – above 5000mg a day (the equivalent of 100 oranges)
– substantially increase the life expectancy of cancer patients.

Yet, despite this, one of the most commonly cited studies is
that from the University of Leicester, which resulted in
newspaper headlines claiming that vitamin supplements cause
cancer.[2] The study in question found that one accepted
marker for oxidative stress and DNA damage – 8-oxoguanine
– decreased with the supplementation of 500mg of vitamin C,
indicating a protective effect. Another less accepted marker,
8-oxadenine, increased. On the basis of this latter finding, the
authors suggested that vitamin C might have a potentially carcinogenic effect. Of course, what the study actually showed
was ambiguous. Vitamin C was shown to be both protective
and harmful to DNA.

According to vitamin C expert, Dr Balz Frei, director of
the Linus Pauling Institute, fears about vitamin C are
unfounded, both because these results contradict the findings
of other research groups and also because poor experimental
procedure could easily have led to oxidative damage to DNA,
which may have been wrongly blamed on vitamin C.
'Frankly, I question whether this data will hold up when we
analyse it further. The value of vitamin C must be considered
in its totality, not just one single biological effect,' says Frei.

Since all anti-oxidants have the potential to become oxidants, once spent, this work may highlight the importance of
nutrient synergy, since sufficient vitamin E, glutathione and
flavonoids help to prolong vitamin C's anti-oxidant effect.
With hundreds of studies concluding that high intakes of vitamin C are associated with lowered cancer risk, there is no

good reason, on the basis of this study involving 30 people, to doubt that vitamin C supplementation remains both safe and effective in preventing cancer.

The moral of these stories is to look at the whole picture and weigh up the totality of the evidence. As the next chapter shows, there is already enough proof that supplementing anti-oxidant nutrients and eating anti-oxidant-rich foods are essential both in preventing cancer and in nutritionally supporting people with the disease.

CHAPTER 20

VITAMINS AND CANCER

Great progress is being made in nutritional approaches to cancer. The discovery that vitamins A, C and E can disarm oxidants, the most prevalent carcinogens, is now the subject of mainstream, government-funded research, into both the treatment and prevention of cancer. To date, results have been very impressive, although we are beginning to understand that the role of a number of anti-cancer agents goes deeper than simply disarming carcinogens.

Vitamin A, for example, not only controls cell growth, but also stimulates communication between cells. Vitamin C boosts immune response in a multitude of ways. Vitamin E protects fats from oxidation and recycles vitamin C. These nutrients are best thought of as 'adaptogens' (substances that help us to adapt to a hostile environment). They are widely available in nature, which suggests a cooperative evolution between us and our natural environment. Many of today's most significant carcinogens are man-made. In other words, they are a consequence of not respecting our relationship with our environment. Cancer may be seen as the result of too many carcinogens and too few adaptogens, leading to a breakdown in communication. Tilting the equation back the other way gives us our best hope of preventing or reversing cancer.

VITAMIN A AND BETA-CAROTENE

Both vitamin A, and its precursor, beta-carotene, have anti-cancer properties. People with lung cancer have been found to have much lower than normal blood vitamin A and carotenoid levels[3] and that there is a strong link between the risk of lung cancer and vitamin A and beta-carotene status. People with low dietary intake of vitamin A have twice the risk of lung cancer as those with the highest vitamin A intake. Similarly, a high intake of beta-carotene from raw fruits and vegetables reduces the risk of lung cancer in smokers[4] and non-smoking men and women,[5] as well as reducing the risk of cancer of the stomach, colon, prostate and cervix.[6]

Evidence for a link between beta-carotene and breast cancer is less strong. One recent study demonstrated that eating plenty of vegetables (which raise carotenoid levels in the blood, increasing fibre levels and reducing dietary fat) did reduce the risk of the recurrence of breast cancer.[7] In another study, which followed over 7000 women for up to nine and a half years, high blood levels of lycopene, a carotenoid which is particularly abundant in tomatoes, was linked to a reduced risk of breast cancer. However, the researchers found no evidence of protection from beta-carotene or vitamin A.[8]

One study supplementing beta-carotene (30mg per day) resulted in the improvement of 71 per cent of patients with oral pre-cancer (leukoplakia), while 200,000iu of vitamin A a day resulted in 57 per cent of patients having complete remission.[9] There is also research on the cancer 'drug' 13-cisretinoic acid (isotretinoin) and all trans-retinoic acid, which is what the body converts vitamin A into. (Retinol is the chemical name for vitamin A.) Dr Huang has shown that all-trans-retinoic acid puts acute myeloid leukemia in complete 'remission'.[10] Drs Hong and Lippman have shown that high doses of 13-cis-retinoic acid have effectively 'suppressed' squamous cell carcinomas of the head and neck.[11] The researchers noted that 'second primary tumours are the chief cause of treatment failure and death in patients' (with head and neck cancers). After a year of treatment of 49 patients with 13-cis-retinoic acid and 51 patients with placebos, 4 per cent had second primary tumours in the 13-cis-retinoic acid group, as opposed to 24 per cent in the placebo group.

These studies are important, not only because they show the value of vitamin A and its metabolites in reversing the cancer process, but also because they do actually look at the metabolites. Even in a person whose blood level of vitamin A is normal, taking supplements can raise levels of these cancer-protecting metabolites. This is the basis of using large doses of vitamin A as part of an anti-cancer regime.

However, vitamin A and its metabolites are not without toxicity. High-dose vitamin A has been shown to increase the risk of birth defects in animals and for this reason it is unwise to supplement more than 10,000iu (3000mcg) if you are pregnant or likely to become pregnant. However, the same caution does not apply to beta-carotene. Although it can be converted into vitamin A, the liver converts very little once the body's vitamin A stores are full, so there is a protective mechanism to guard against taking in too much. Since beta-carotene is an anti-oxidant and anti-cancer agent in its own right, having more of it circulating around the body is definitely good news.

An ideal daily supplemental intake of vitamin A is 5000–10,000iu and 15–25mg of beta-carotene, in addition to eating a high fruit and vegetable diet. Larger intakes may be appropriate for people with cancer but these should only be given with proper guidance and monitoring by your health practitioner.

The consistent link between a high dietary intake and sufficient levels in the blood of beta-carotene and vitamin A and a low risk for cancer are good enough reasons to eat foods rich in this key nutrient (see over) and to top up with supplements. However, much more research needs to be done to identify the actual role of beta-carotene in the treatment of cancer.

Which foods are best for vitamin A and beta-carotene?

Foods are listed in order of those that contain the most beta-carotene or vitamin A per calorie of food. The figures in brackets are the amount of beta-carotene or vitamin A in 100g, which is roughly equivalent to a cup or serving.

Beef liver	(35,778iu)	Broccoli	(1541iu)
Veal liver	(26,562iu)	Apricots (fresh)	(2612iu)
Carrots	(28,125iu)	Papayas	(2014iu)
Watercress	(4700iu)	Asparagus	(829iu)
Cabbage	(3000iu)	Apricots (dried)	(7240iu)
Squash	(7000iu)	Peppers	(530iu)
Sweet potatoes	(17,055iu)	Tangerines	(920iu)
Melon	(3224iu)	Nectarines	(730iu)
Pumpkin	(1600iu)	Peaches	(535iu)
Mangoes	(3894iu)	Watermelon	(365iu)
Tomatoes	(1133iu)		

VITAMIN C

In 1991, Dr Gladys Block, formerly with the National Cancer Institute, published a review[12] of studies linking vitamin C with cancer prevention which concludes:

Approximately 90 epidemiologic studies have examined the role of vitamin C or vitamin-C-rich foods in cancer prevention, and the vast majority have found statistically significant protective effects. Evidence is strong for cancers of the oesophagus, oral cavity, stomach and pancreas. There is also substantial evidence of a protective effect in cancers of the cervix, rectum and breast. Even in lung cancer there is recent evidence of a role for vitamin C.

Like beta-carotene, the overwhelming evidence is that a high intake of vitamin C correlates with a low risk for cancer. Another review of vitamin C research reached similar conclusions: 'Epidemiologic evidence of a protective effect of vitamin C for non-hormone cancers is very strong. Of the 46 such studies in which a dietary vitamin C index was calculated, 33 found statistically significant protection.'

The first ever study in which vitamin C was given to cancer patients was carried out in the 1970s, by Dr Linus Pauling and Dr Ewan Cameron, a cancer specialist, working in Scotland. They gave 100 terminally ill cancer patients 10g (10,000mg) of vitamin C each day and compared their outcome with 1000 cancer patients given conventional therapy. The survival rate was five times higher in those taking vitamin C and, by 1978, while all of the 1000 'control patients' had died, 13 of the vitamin C patients were still alive, with 12 apparently free from cancer.[13] More recent studies have confirmed these findings. Drs Murata and Morishige of Saga University in Japan showed that cancer patients on 5–30g of vitamin C lived six times longer than those on 4g or less, while those suffering from cancer of the uterus lived 15 times longer on vitamin C therapy.[14] This was also confirmed by Dr Abram Hoffer in Canada who found that patients on high doses of vitamin C survived, on average, ten times longer.

However, Pauling and Cameron's findings were discredited, largely due to an apparent 'replication' of their study by the Mayo Clinic in the US.[15] There was, however, one major difference between the original trial and that of the Mayo Clinic. The 'terminal' patients in the original trial kept taking vitamin C every day, while those in the Mayo Clinic trial stopped after an average of 75 days. However, by then, the book was closed and mega-dose vitamin C was considered quackery.

Of all the anti-oxidants, vitamin C is the most extraordinary. Vitamin C is believed to help prevent and treat cancer by enhancing the immune system; stimulating the formation of collagen which is necessary for 'walling off' tumours; preventing metastasis (spreading) by keeping the ground substance around tumours intact, by inhibiting a particular enzyme; preventing viruses that can cause cancer; correcting a vitamin C deficiency which is often seen in cancer patients; speeding up wound healing in cancer patients after surgery; enhancing the effectiveness of some chemotherapy drugs; reducing the toxicity of some chemotherapy; preventing free radical damage and neutralising some carcinogens.

Numerous studies have found a link between vitamin C intake and the incidence of several different cancers, especially non-hormonal cancers.[16] The evidence for the benefits of vitamin C is strongest for cancers of the mouth, oesophagus, stomach, lung, pancreas and cervix. While one analysis of 12 clinical studies found that, 'Vitamin C intake had the most consistent and statistically significant inverse association with breast cancer risk,'[17] the evidence of an associated decreased risk for breast cancer is not as strong. One study involving 34,000 post-menopausal women, reported no association between the intake of vitamins A, C and E and a reduced risk of developing breast cancer.[18]

The WCRF (World Cancer Research Fund) conclude that there is no evidence of a relationship between vitamin C intake and prostate cancer and insufficient evidence for breast cancer. The studies to date do suggest a big difference between the causes and treatment of hormone-related cancers and those of the lung or digestive tract. These lung and digestive tract cancers may be more related to oxidant carcinogens, and prevented by increasing one's intake of anti-oxidant nutrients.

Overall, the research to date strongly supports the importance of eating a diet rich in vitamin C (see over). While supplementing 1–5g vitamin C may help prevent some cancers, cancer patients are most likely to benefit from 10 grams or more a day. These higher levels are best taken with the guidance of your health practitioner.

Which foods are best for vitamin C?

Foods are listed in order of those that contain the most vitamin C per calorie of food. The figures in brackets are the amount of vitamin C in 100g, which is roughly equivalent to a cup or serving.

Peppers	(100mg)	Papayas	(62mg)
Watercress	(60mg)	Peas	(25mg)
Cabbage	(60mg)	Melons	(25mg)
Broccoli	(110mg)	Oranges	(50mg)
Cauliflower	(60mg)	Grapefruits	(40mg)
Strawberries	(60mg)	Limes	(29mg)
Lemons	(80mg)	Tomatoes	(60mg)
Kiwi fruit	(85mg)	Tangerines	(31mg)
Brussels sprouts	(62mg)	Mangoes	(28mg)

VITAMIN E

While vitamin C is a water-based anti-oxidant, protecting the watery parts of the body, vitamin E is a fat-based anti-oxidant so it protects cell membranes and structural fats. Having a low level of vitamin E in your blood significantly increases your risk of both smoking-related and other cancers, according to a Finnish study which studied 21,172 men for ten years.[19] Further evidence for vitamin E's potent protective role against cancer was shown in an analysis of 59 clinical studies. The researchers found that there was 'modest' protection from vitamin supplements, but vitamin E supplements were most consistently associated with a reduced risk of cancer.[20]

Vitamin E deficiency is, however, most strongly associated with an increased risk of breast cancer. Research in 1984 in Britain, led by Dr Wald at St Bartholomew's Hospital in London, found that 'Those with the lowest vitamin E levels have the highest risk for breast cancer'.[21] A more recent trial, involving 2569 women with breast cancer, concluded, 'A diet rich in several micronutrients, especially beta-carotene, vitamin E and calcium, may be protective against breast cancer'.[22] These are but a few examples from a wealth of data that links breast cancer with low vitamin E levels, and prevention of breast cancer with increased vitamin E intake.

While there is plenty of evidence showing the anti-oxidant role that vitamin E itself can play in the prevention of breast cancer, a recent study has confirmed similar benefit from tocotrienols, which are in the same chemical 'family' as vitamin E. Tocotrienols have been found to work in tandem with vitamin E in inhibiting the growth of breast cancer cells in humans. They are found in significant concentrations in palm oil, barley extracts and rice oil.[23]

Vitamin E supplementation has also been shown to help protect against prostate cancer. A study on Finnish men, published in the *Journal of the National Cancer Institute*, showed a 41 per cent lower death rate from prostate cancer in those supplementing vitamin E. The men who took 50mg of vitamin E daily for five to eight years had a 32 per cent lower rate of symptomatic prostate cancer than men who did not take the supplement. 'This intriguing observation suggests that vitamin E has the potential to prevent one of the most common malignant tumours in the North American and European populations,' according to researcher Dr Olli Heinonen from the University of Helsinki, who believes that vitamin E's anti-oxidant properties may help stave off prostate cancer by fighting oxidants and boosting the immune system.[24]

Another study, involving 29,133 male smokers, found that 32 per cent fewer of those supplementing vitamin E developed prostate cancer and the mortality rate from the disease was 41 per cent lower.[25]

An optimal supplemental intake for cancer prevention is between 400 and 800iu (270 and 540mg) per day, on top of eating foods rich in vitamin E (see over).

Which foods are best for vitamin E?

Foods are listed in order of those that contain the most vitamin E per calorie of food. The figures in brackets are the amount of vitamin E in 100g, which is roughly equivalent to a cup or serving.

Cold-pressed seed oil	(83mg)	Salmon	(1.8mg)
Sunflower seeds	(52.6mg)	Sweet potato	(4.0mg)
Peanuts	(11.8mg)	Almonds	(24.5mg)
Sesame seeds	(22.7mg)	Walnuts	(19.6mg)
Beans	(7.7mg)	Pecans	(19.8mg)
Peas	(2.3mg)	Cashews	(10.9mg)
Wheatgerm	(27.5mg)	Brown rice	(2.0mg)
Tuna	(6.3mg)	Lentils	(1.3mg)
Sardines	(2.0mg)		

OTHER ANTI-CANCER VITAMINS

Many other vitamins are immune-boosting and potentially helpful in reducing cancer risk. Of the B vitamins, vitamin B6, B12 and folic acid are very important for the immune system. A recent study showed that dietary intake of folic acid was associated with a reduced risk of the recurrence of colon cancer.[26]

Vitamin D, long thought to be only important for bone health, may also help reduce risk for breast and colon cancer. It has long been known that women who live in sunnier countries are less likely to develop the disease than women who see little sunshine, but it has now been found that women who have high levels of vitamin D are more likely to survive if they do. Vitamin D is made by a process which involves the exposure of skin to sunlight.

This theory, first proposed by Dr Cedrick Garland in 1980, led to research that showed a strong association between risk for colon cancer and dietary intake of vitamin D and calcium.[27] An eight-year study of 25,802 people from the state of

Maryland found that those with blood levels of vitamin D equivalent to 400iu (10mcg) or more had half the risk of colon cancer of those with lower levels.[28] And scientists at Manchester University have recently reported that women with advanced breast cancer that had spread to their bones were less likely to die of the disease when they had high amounts of active vitamin D in their blood.[29] One possible explanation for the cancer-protective effect of vitamin D is that calcium is important for proper immune function. Vitamin D helps the body to make use of calcium. In any event, the presence of both nutrients in optimal amounts equates with a lower risk for colon and breast cancer.

GLUTATHIONE

Glutathione is not a vitamin, but deserves attention as it is perhaps the most important anti-oxidant within cells and has proven to be highly cancer-protective. It is like a protein (being made out of three amino acids) and, as well as being an anti-oxidant in its own right, is also part of key anti-oxidant enzymes such as glutathione peroxidase and glutathione trans-ferase. It can also recycle vitamin C, multiplying its ability to promote our health. It plays a major role in detoxifying the body and protecting us against the harmful effects of carcino-gens, especially oxidants and radiation. In addition, it protects DNA and cell growth.[30] In short, it fits the description of an all-round cancer-protective agent. Low levels are found in cancer patients.

Recent studies indicate that glutathione may have an important role to play in both the prevention and treatment of cancer, as it helps to kill cancer cells by improving the body's natural immunity.[31] Glutathione is normally made in the body from the amino acid cysteine, found in a variety of foods (especially garlic). Supplementing it on its own is mildly effective, but the problem is that the glutathione sacrifices itself to protect the body from oxidants. Glutathione is already included in several chemotherapy drugs.

The recent discovery that glutathione was effectively recycled by anthocyanidins, found in grapes, berries and beetroot, led to a new anti-cancer approach of combining glutathione with anthocyanidins, thereby substantially increasing the power of this key anti-oxidant.[32] Human trials are now underway, using a supplement called Recancostat Compositum, available in Germany, and early results are encouraging. One trial involves 11 people with advanced colorectal cancer, having completed two chemotherapy treatments and given little chance of survival.[33] Three died early in the trial. Of the remaining eight, four have made remarkable improvement. All are continuing on this potentially important therapy, which has proven to be non-toxic.

In the UK, a supplement called Rejuvan Forté, a combination of glutathione and anthocyanidins, is available (see Useful Addresses) and it is recommended as part of an overall immune-boosting strategy. The ideal dose is three tablets per day.

CO-ENZYME Q10 (UBIQUINONE)

Co-enzyme Q10 (Co-Q) is not classified as a vitamin because we can make it in the body. Co-Q is a vital anti-oxidant, helping to protect cells from carcinogens and also helping to recycle vitamin E. There is evidence that Co-Q levels are lower than normal in people with cancer[34] and that the need for Co-Q increases when you have the disease. For this reason, researchers are now considering giving extra Co-Q to combat cancer. The first cases to be reported are of women with breast cancer treated in Denmark. Out of 36 women classified as 'high risk', since their tumours had spread, six patients showed 'apparent partial remission' following the supplementation of 90mg of Co-Q, together with other anti-oxidants.[35] An additional three women treated with 390mg of Co-Q have also shown apparent remission.[36] These results are encouraging and highlight the potential importance of supplementing this nutrient to ensure optimal levels.

SYNERGY – THE WHOLE IS GREATER THAN THE SUM OF ITS PARTS

None of these nutrients works in isolation in the body, nor are people ever deficient in just one nutrient. As good as the results discussed so far appear, they underestimate the power of optimum nutrition in preventing and reversing the cancer process.

Vitamin C, which is water-soluble, and vitamin E, fat-soluble, are synergistic: together they can protect the tissues and fluids in the body. What's more, when vitamin E has 'disarmed' a carcinogen, the vitamin E can be 'reloaded' by vitamin C, so their combined presence in the diet and the body has a synergistic effect.

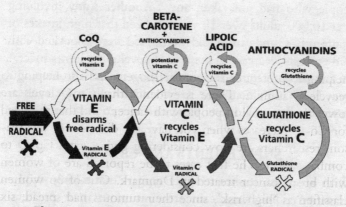

Figure 8 – The synergistic action of nutrients in disarming a free radical

The same is true of selenium and vitamin E. When these nutrients are provided together, the level of cancer protection is considerably multiplied. For example, another study from Finland, carried out by Dr Jukka Salonen and colleagues at the University of Kuopio on 12,000 people over several years, found that those in the top third of both vitamin E and selenium blood levels had a 91 per cent decreased risk of cancer compared to those in the bottom third.[37] Having high levels of both these nutrients gave them less than one-tenth the risk of those with sub-optimal levels.

Vitamins C and E are also a powerful anti-cancer combination. A ten-year study on over 11,000 people, completed in 1996, found that those supplementing both vitamin C and vitamin E halved their overall risk of death from all cancers.[38]

One study in Seattle involving over 800 people who took a multivitamin supplement daily was associated with halving the risk of developing colon cancer. The nutrients linked to the decreased risk were vitamins A, C, E, folic acid and the mineral calcium. The strongest link was with vitamin E – people who supplemented at least 200iu of vitamin E over ten years had 57 per cent less chance of getting colon cancer than people who had not taken any.[39] Another study involving over 10,000 adults over 19 years showed that high intakes of vitamins E, C and carotenoids combined were associated with a 68 per cent decrease in the risk of developing lung cancer.[40] An animal study found the combination of beta-carotene, vitamin E, C and glutathione to be substantially more cancer-protective than any one of these nutrients in isolation.[41]

SUPPLEMENTS AND CANCER

All in all, these studies strongly suggest that taking supplements providing significant amounts of vitamin A, beta-carotene, vitamin C and E, plus vitamin D and B vitamins, is likely, at the very least, to halve your risk of cancer. Dr

Richard Passwater, who first identified the synergistic relationship between vitamin C and E and has spent the past 30 years researching anti-oxidant nutrients and cancer, believes that supplementation combined with an appropriate diet could cut your risk of cancer to a quarter.

The chart below shows which nutrients have proven most effective against which kind of cancer.

Which nutrient for which type of cancer?

The following anti-oxidant vitamins and minerals have so far been proved effective in medical research against the types of cancer indicated.

Type	Vitamin A	Beta-carotene	Vitamin C	Vitamin E	Selenium
Bladder		★			★
Breast		★	★	★	★
Cervix	★		★	★	
Colon	★	★	★		★
Head and neck	★	★			
HIV-related			★		
Kidney			★		
Leukaemia			★		★
Liver					★
Lung	★	★	★	★	★
Lymphoma	★				
Oesophagus			★		★
Oral	★	★	★		★
Pancreas			★		
Prostate	★				★
Skin	★		★		
Stomach	★		★	★	★

CHAPTER 21

MINERALS AND CANCER

Like vitamins, minerals are also essential for the immune system. Key minerals for healthy immunity include calcium, magnesium, zinc and selenium. Of these, selenium stands out as as an important ally in the fight against cancer.

Selenium has long been known to protect against cancer. Numerous studies have linked a lower intake of dietary selenium to an increased risk of cancer. For example, in one study conducted on 4480 men from the US, those who at the start of the study had selenium levels in the lowest fifth were twice as likely to develop cancer as those in the highest fifth.[42] Studies in China confirmed the same phenomenon — that those with low selenium levels in the blood (below 8mcg per dl) had three times the risk of cancer as those with high blood levels (above 11mcg per dl).[43]

One recent study showed that people who lived in areas with low soil selenium and had supplemented 200mcg of selenium for four and a half years had a reduced risk of developing cancer. Although the supplementation did not appear to reduce the incidence of skin cancer, total cancers, as well as lung, colorectal and prostate cancers were significantly lower.[44] Few people take in even a quarter of this amount (200mcg) and there is evidence that dietary intake and blood levels of selenium are falling in the Western world. In Britain the Ministry of Agriculture, Fisheries and Food estimate that the average intake is now 35mcg a day, compared to 60mcg in 1975. Current low levels of selenium could be a contributing factor to cancer as well as other health problems such as cardiovascular disease.[45]

Selenium, like other anti-oxidant nutrients, has a positive role to play at many stages in the cancer process. It protects genes from damage, helps cells use oxygen efficiently, and appears to slow down cell division (resulting in fewer errors as new cells are made). It can also help detoxify a wide variety of carcinogens by improving liver function; the liver is the body's main dextoxifying organ.[46]

SUPPLEMENTING SELENIUM

Following animal studies that found selenium protecting against a number of cancers,[47] a number of human trials have now been published that show the importance of this mineral. In one trial, Dr Larry Clark, and colleagues at Cornell University, gave one group of people 200mcg of selenium and another group a placebo. They found a significant reduction in the incidence of lung, colorectal and prostate cancer and a reduced mortality from lung cancer amongst the selenium group.[48]

Studies in the region of Quidong in China, where liver cancer rates are among the highest in the world, have found a strong correlation between low selenium intake and cancer risk. Other risk factors are hepatitis-B infection, exposure to the dietary carcinogen aflatoxin and a genetic predisposition. Scientists then began a large-scale selenium study in which an entire village of 20,000 people supplemented selenium which was added to their salt. In the following years there was a significant drop in the incidence of hepatitis-B and in incidence of liver cancer.[49]

A seven-nation, $30 million trial into the impact of selenium on cancer is now underway. The United Kingdom,

Finland, Norway, Sweden, Denmark, the Netherlands and the USA are each recruiting around 7500 subjects to receive varying amounts of selenium or a placebo over a six-year period.

With average dietary intakes of selenium often below 50mcg and optimal levels four times higher than this, most cancer experts recommend supplementing 100–200mcg of selenium (as selenomethionine or selenocysteine), as well as eating foods rich in the mineral. Generally, foods rich in selenium include seafood, wholefoods, nuts and seeds (especially Brazil nuts and sesame seeds). In practice (with the exception of seafood), the level of selenium in foods reflects the level of selenium in the soil in which they are grown. It is highly likely that continued intensive farming will lead to selenium depletion in soil and therefore in plants.

OTHER MINERALS

As with vitamins, minerals work in synergy and the best disease prevention strategy is probably an all-round optimal intake of minerals. Apart from selenium, zinc, calcium and magnesium are especially important for immune function.

Calcium, particularly in conjunction with other micronutrients, has also been associated with a reduced risk of cancer, particularly of the breast and colon.[50] A 15-year study in Sweden found that a high intake of calcium reduced the risk of colon cancer.[51] In animals, having a high intake of calcium and vitamin D significantly reduces the risk of breast cancer.[52] Vitamin D is known to help the body use calcium which is a vital nutrient for healthy immunity.

The level of zinc found in people with prostate cancer has been shown to be significantly lower than normal.[53] Also, the toxic element cadmium, which is a known zinc antagonist, can stimulate growth of prostate tissue and is therefore considered a carcinogen. Cadmium is found in cigarettes and in exhaust fumes, as well as galvanised pipes and – depending on your plumbing – in some household water supplies. Not smoking and ensuring an optimal zinc intake is the best way to protect against cadmium. No studies to date have looked at the therapeutic role of treating cancer with zinc. An optimal intake of zinc is 15–20mg a day, which is two to three times the average daily intake. Seeds and nuts and 'seed' foods such as wholegrains (which contain the seed), peas, broad beans, lentils and beans are rich in zinc.

CHAPTER 22

HERBS AND NATURAL CANCER REMEDIES

Many plants and plant extracts have powerful immune-boosting properties and have been shown to influence different stages of the cancer process. These include aloe vera, cat's claw, echinacea, sheep's sorrel, garlic, various mushrooms and numerous natural sources of anti-oxidants including berry extracts, silymarin from milk thistle, and pycnogenol from pine bark. This is by no means a comprehensive list. However, each of these plants and extracts have been demonstrated either to increase the odds against cancer or significantly boost the immune system. Unlike vitamins and minerals they are not classified as 'essential nutrients'. But they may play an important part in a comprehensive anti-cancer strategy, aimed at supporting the immune system.

ESSIAC

One popular herbal cancer remedy is Essiac – a herbal blend based on a recipe from the Ojibwa people in Canada and developed by a nurse, Rene Caisse, in the 1920s. Indeed, she administered Essiac to her 72-year-old mother when she was diagnosed with inoperable liver cancer; her mother died just after her ninetieth birthday, without pain, 'of a tired heart'. Its history has been tumultuous, in the face of much opposition from parts of the medical establishment.

Essiac is formulated from four herbs – sheep's sorrel (*Rumex acetosa*), burdock (*Arctium lappa*), Indian rhubarb (*Rheum palmatum*) and slippery elm (*Ulmus fulva*). Sheep's sorrel was shown in one study to have strong anti-tumour activity and other immune-boosting properties.[54] It also contains several vitamins and minerals. Burdock has been shown to reduce cell mutation.[55] It also contains inulin, which is a powerful immune stimulant. Indian rhubarb is also an immune-booster; it helps cleanse the liver of toxic wastes and improves the supply of oxygen to tissues. Slippery elm is rich in many vitamins and minerals and helps support mucous membranes. Essiac is mixed and drunk as a liquid – initially 60ml twice a day. See Useful Addresses for stockists.

CAT'S CLAW (*UNCARIA TOMENTOSA*)

Cat's claw is a woody vine that can wind its way over 100 feet up through the trees in its attempt to reach light in the Peruvian rainforests – its thorn is shaped like the claw of a cat. The native Indians have long used its bark to treat cancer.

Although research is still in its early stages, results so far have been so convincing that the plant has become an endangered species and in 1989 the Peruvian government banned the harvesting and use of the root of the two main species (*U. tomentosa* and *U. guianensis*). However, it appears that the bark also contains most or all of the medicinal properties.

Components of cat's claw have been shown to increase the ability of white blood cells to carry out phagocytosis (i.e. to engulf, digest and so destroy misbehaving cells). It also contains other chemicals which reduce inflammation. It is potentially a super-plant, with immune-stimulating, anti-oxidant, anti-inflammatory, anti-tumour and anti-microbial properties. Austrian researchers have also identified extracts which they have been using to treat cancer and viral infections.[56] One problem they have come across is that different samples contain different amounts of these therapeutic chemicals, which makes dosage difficult to calculate; it is not yet known whether this is due to location, season or species variation.

Cat's claw comes either as capsules, with 2g being a good daily dose, or as tea (loose or in tea bags). A 2g dose is probably equivalent to two cups a day. You can get more out of the loose tea by boiling it for 5 minutes and then adding a little blackcurrant and apple juice concentrate to improve the taste.

ECHINACEA

This root of *Echinacea purpurea* (purple coneflower) is probably the most widely used immune-boosting herb. It possesses interferon-like properties and contains special kinds of polysaccharides, such as inulin, which increase macrophage production. These have been shown to destroy cancer cells in test tube experiments. One study, on a group of healthy men, found that after five days of taking 30 drops of Echinacea extract, three times a day, their white blood cells had doubled their 'phagocytic' power.[57] Whether Echinacea's immune-boosting properties are maintained over a long period of time is not yet known. Some researchers recommend just using it to boost immunity when your health is actually under threat.

Echinacea is best taken either as capsules of the powdered herb (2000mg a day) or as drops of a concentrated extract, usually 20 drops three times a day.

ALOE VERA

Another source of special polysaccharides is aloe vera. While it contains numerous beneficial substances, including vitamins, minerals, amino acids, essential fats and enzymes, probably its most potent substance is acemannan. This extract has been proven to improve immune power by increasing numbers and function of T-cells and macrophages.[58] Aloe vera is usually taken as a concentration of the juice. Check the potency carefully – there's a wide variation. Look for the quantity of MPSs (mucopolysaccharides) – reputable companies will provide this information.

HEALING MUSHROOMS

Certain kinds of mushrooms have been used for years in China and Japan for their immune-boosting properties. The most popular are Ganoderma (reishi), shiitake and maitake.

Shiitake mushrooms contain another special polysaccharide called lentinan which also boosts immune function. Extracts of the maitake mushroom have shown encouraging results in helping to treat cancer. Researchers in Japan found that giving maitake helped tumours regress in two-thirds of patients with breast, lung and liver cancer. They also found that if maitake was taken in conjunction with chemotherapy, response rates rose from 12 to 28 per cent. In this study, maitake was not shown to be as effective against bone and stomach cancers or leukaemia.[59] The immune-boosting benefits of the reishi mushroom (*Ganoderma lucidum*) are becoming increasingly evident. One study in Taiwan showed an extract of the mushroom to have anti-tumour properties[60] and another demonstrated its anti-oxidant effects.[61]

All these mushrooms are available as powders, with the therapeutic dose being 500mg three times a day. Many are also included in natural remedies designed to support healthy immunity. However, shiitake mushrooms are now sold fresh in better supermarkets, and dried in most healthfood stores. They are delicious and, as a regular part of your diet, strengthen your immune system.

Another interesting herb that is often used in conjunction with these anti-cancer mushrooms in China is astragalus. Astragalus has been proven to increase T-cell count and function and to protect the immune system from radiation and harmful chemicals including chemotherapy.[62]

GARLIC

Garlic is especially rich in the sulphur-containing amino acids, glutathione and cysteine, which are powerful anti-oxidants. Not only does it protect against the formation of tumours, including metastases, it also inhibits the growth of established tumours, strengthening the immune system and detoxifying the liver. A National Cancer Institute study carried out in China in 1989 found that provinces which used garlic liberally had the lowest rate of stomach cancer.[63] The results of a large study involving 41,837 women aged between 55 and 69 from Iowa, USA, indicated that garlic was the most protective type of vegetable against colon cancer. Women who said they ate garlic at least once a week were 50 per cent less likely to contract colon cancer than those who said they never ate it.[64] One to three cloves a day, or the equivalent in capsules, provides good support for the immune system and may help protect against cancer.

PLANT ANTI-OXIDANTS

There are literally hundreds of plant anti-oxidants which is no doubt one big reason why eating plenty of fruit and vegetables is so strongly connected with significant reductions in cancer risk. Many are responsible for the different colours of plants, for example, purple, red, orange, yellow and green. Among these, anthocyanidins and proanthocyanidins are found in fruits with a red/blue hue including berries and grapes, as well as beetroot. These are especially important as they can potentiate the effect of glutathione, a key cellular anti-oxidant (see page 124). Taken with glutathione, they have proved to be highly cancer-protective.

Grape seed extract is very rich in anti-oxidants which have been shown to have a protective effect against cancer. In one study a particular extract was found to inhibit a key enzyme involved in cell division by up to 50 per cent. Cancer cells spread by dividing rapidly.[65] In animal studies anthocyanidins have been shown to suppress the growth of tumours.[66]

Carotenoids, such as beta-carotene in carrots and lycopene in tomatoes, are also powerful anti-oxidants and anti-cancer agents. Other anti-oxidants known to be cancer-protective include silymarin. One study has shown that silymarin, a component of the milk thistle plant, can protect against some forms of cancer in mice.[67] In a test tube experiment on human breast cancer cells, silymarin was shown to inhibit cell growth.[68] Also important are flavonoids, such as those found in citrus fruit, pycnogenol from pine bark and quercitin from cranberry. Turmeric, the main spice in curry, is a powerful anti-oxidant and anti-inflammatory agent and is showing remarkable anti-cancer properties in clinical trials. It has been shown to protect against every stage of cancer development – initiation, promotion and progression.[69] It also disarms a wide range of carcinogens. The active ingredient is almost certainly curcumin and there is little doubt that, as research unfolds, curcumin will be seen as an important natural anti-cancer agent.

We can take in significant amounts of these plant anti-oxidants simply by eating a diet rich in fruits and vegetables, especially by eating something orange or red every day, such as carrots and tomatoes, and something red or blue such as berries. Many of these phytonutrients are found in advanced anti-oxidant supplements and those supplement formulas designed to support the immune system.

SHARK CARTILAGE

Once a cancer mass is formed it develops its own blood supply and defence system. This process is called angiogenesis. It then becomes increasingly difficult for the immune system to deal with the tumour, which now has a life of its own. One strategy, known as anti-angiogenesis, is to cut off the tumour's blood supply so that it effectively starves to death. In 1976 Dr Robert Langer, of the Massachusetts Institute of Technology, discovered an inhibitor of new blood vessels in tumours – shark cartilage. As cartilage has no blood supply it makes sense that it would contain such an inhibitor. While different kinds of cartilage have been shown to have anti-tumour properties, shark cartilage has proven the most effective to date. This may also explain why the incidence of cancer in sharks, who have no bones, is less than 1 per cent of that of other fish.

Unlike nutritional strategies, which have been tested more for preventing cancer, shark cartilage has been tested in advanced cancer for inducing its remission. Leading its research is Dr William Lane, author of *Sharks Don't Get Cancer* (see Recommended Reading). To date, trials have been small, but positive. In eight breast cancer cases where the tumours were as large as golf balls in size, all eight women were virtually tumour-free after 11 weeks of taking shark cartilage. In another study by a New Jersey doctor, 76 cancer patients all responded well to shark cartilage. A liquid extract of shark cartilage, marketed as the drug Neovastat, is entering the final stages of clinical trials. Many studies are now under way and the results are awaited with interest.

The shark cartilage approach is applicable for treatment of cancer, rather than its prevention, and, to be most effective, must be used in doses as high as 60g per day for solid tumours.

LAETRILE

Laetrile, an extract from the apricot kernel, has often been used in aggressive anti-cancer strategies. It acts more like chemotherapy, and is claimed to target only the cancer cells.

When laetrile is broken down by the body, one of its components is cyanide. Normal, non-cancerous cells contain an enzyme that converts this to thiocyanate, a non-toxic substance used by the body to make vitamin B12 (cyanocobalamin). Cancer cells lack this enzyme and are effectively poisoned. Another breakdown product of laetrile – benzoic acid – is said to act as a natural painkiller.

The California Medical Association were critical of its value as an anti-cancer substance, although their report did state: 'All the physicians whose patients were reviewed spoke of an increase in the sense of well-being and appetite, gain in weight and decrease in pain.' It continues to be used, with reported success, as part of various natural anti-cancer regimes. Like shark cartilage, it is not a necessary part of a prevention strategy.

SPECIALISED ANTI-CANCER DIET REGIMES

A number of specialised anti-cancer diet strategies have been reported over the years, all applying many of the key dietary principles in this book, each with their own combination of supplemental therapies. Most famous is the Gerson diet, based on the work of Dr Max Gerson, who treated hundreds of so-called terminal cases with a reported 50 per cent recovery rate. His regime included taking pancreatic enzymes, vitamin B12 injections and following a diet, plus enemas designed to detoxify the liver.

Dr W.D. Kelly in the US cured himself of cancer, having been given one month to live and went on to specialise in treating cancer patients. Like Gerson, his regime also supplemented pancreatic enzymes and emphasised detoxifying the body.

Dr Hans Neiper, a German cancer therapist, also reported success with terminal patients using high doses of enzymes such as bromelain, the idea being that this rich source of protein-digesting enzymes can help to weaken cancer masses. One French study, involving 12 patients with cancer, showed impressive results with 600mg of bromelain a day.[70]

Dr Johanna Budwig emphasised the importance of flax oil, while Dr A. Ferenczi in Hungary recommended a kilogram of beetroot every day, now known to be an exceedingly rich source of anthocyanidins.

In Britain, the Bristol Cancer Centre pioneered a holistic approach incorporating a mixture of different strategies including counselling. There are also a number of clinics in Mexico, where restrictions on treating cancer are less stringent than in the US. Many advocate very large doses of vitamins, especially vitamin C, and often use laetrile. Some use hydrazine sulphate, a liver enzyme which conserves energy for the patient by converting the lactic acid produced by a tumour back into glucose (normally this is a reaction that takes much more energy from the patient than it generates). Some also use 'oxygen therapy' – different ways of helping to oxygenate body tissues.

It is not within the scope of this book to give detailed descriptions or make judgements on these different approaches. Most have not been proven in extensive medical trials although many of them report exciting anecdotal results. All focus on detoxifying the body and promoting its ability to fight back. For people with particularly malignant types of cancer, for which conventional treatment has proven unsuccessful, they certainly represent an alternative approach worthy of consideration, with the guidance of your health practitioner.

PART 5

HOW TO AVOID CANCER

....

CHAPTER 23

THE IDEAL DIET

On the basis of all the evidence presented in this book, you now know what you need to eat and drink (or not) to minimise your risk of cancer. This chapter spells it out in two ways. First, there's a list of foods and drinks to increase and to decrease, giving you ideal targets to aim at. Then there are practical suggestions about which foods to eat.

These suggestions can help you prevent and reverse the cancer process. Depending on your current eating habits and tastes, you may find the changes hard to achieve at first. But once you start making realistic steps towards your goal, you will be making progress.

At the end of the chapter there's a typical day's menu incorporating all the beneficial foods to show how you can enjoy your food *and* eat yourself to health.

There are many, many different dishes you can concoct using foods that reduce your risk. Of all the foods and principles we've discussed, probably the most important ones are to eat at least five servings of fruits and vegetables a day (organic if possible), cut back on meat (choosing fish or soya products instead), reduce alcohol and avoid frying. You can 'steam-fry' instead, by adding a watery sauce to a panful of, say vegetables and tofu, putting the lid on tight and steaming in the sauce.

THE ANTI-CANCER DIET

Foods and drinks to decrease

- Avoid or at least limit your intake of red meat to a maximum of 80g (3 oz) a day.

- Avoid or rarely eat burnt meat – be it grilled, fried or barbecued.

- Minimise your intake of fried food. Boil, steam, poach or bake food instead.

- Limit your intake of dairy food, choosing organic whenever possible.

- Don't drink alcohol and, if you do, certainly limit your intake to two drinks a day. Ideally, limit your intake to three or four drinks a week, preferably choosing red wine.

Foods and drinks to increase

- When you eat it, choose organic low-fat meat, game or free-range chicken.

- Eat fish, such as herring, mackerel, salmon or tuna, instead of red meat.

- Eat plenty of fruit and vegetables – at least five servings a day (organic whenever possible).

- Have a variety of 'colours' of fruits and vegetables, including something orange every day (such as carrots, sweet potato, tomatoes, peaches or melons) and something red/purple (such as berries, grapes or beetroot).

- Have a serving of cruciferous vegetable every day. This includes broccoli, Brussels sprouts, cabbage, cauliflower and kale.

- Have a clove or two of garlic every day. Choose shiitake mushrooms and spice up dishes with turmeric. These all contain anti-cancer agents.

- Have some soya milk or tofu every other day.

- Add flax seeds to your breakfast and use flax seed oil in salad dressings. Generally avoid refined vegetable oils – use only cold-pressed oils.

- Eat wholefoods, such as wholegrains, lentils, beans, nuts, seeds and vegetables, all of which contain fibre. Some of the fibre in vegetables is destroyed by cooking so it's good to eat something raw every day.

- Drink green tea and 'red' herb teas, rich in anti-oxidants, or regular tea, in preference to coffee. However, for general health, don't drink excessive amounts of either.

- Instead drink six glasses of water, diluted juice, or herb and fruit teas each day. An excellent choice would be cat's claw tea sweetened with blackcurrant and apple concentrate.

A TYPICAL ANTI-CANCER MENU

BREAKFAST
Immune berry booster
*A delicious, textured blend of yoghurt,
berries, wheatgerm and seeds.*

OR

Oat muesli with berries
*A hearty, healthy breakfast full of variety –
oats, berries, yoghurt and more.*

OR

Super oats
Filling and full of flavour – oats with fruit and seeds.

MID-MORNING SNACK
A piece of fruit

LUNCH
Winter warmer Soup
A chunky vegetable soup
OR
Carrot soup in the raw
Carrots and other ingredients, blended raw and heated gently to serve.
OR
Rainbow root salad
A wonderfully colourful mixture of carrot, cabbage, parsnip and beetroot in a tangy vinaigrette.
OR
Recovery soup
Vegetables and tofu, seasoned and blended cold, then heated to serve.
OR
Carrot and sweet potato soup
Flavoured with a hint of coconut – warming and delicious.

MID-AFTERNOON SNACK
Watermelon protection or berry juice cocktail
Great, tasty shakes.

DINNER
Thai-style buckwheat noodles with shiitake mushrooms
Shiitake mushrooms and tofu sautéed in spices, served on very nutritious noodles.
OR
Salmon with mashed sweet potato and Brussels sprouts in a hummus and mushroom sauce
Speaks for itself – a gourmet meal.
OR
Fish stew with artichokes and oyster mushrooms
A delicious, thick stew, brimming with goodness too.

RECIPES

Breakfast

IMMUNE BERRY BOOSTER

SERVES 1

150g (5 oz) low-fat live yoghurt
100g (4 oz) berries (strawberries, blueberries, raspberries, blackcurrants)
1 tablespoon wheatgerm
1 tablespoon mixed ground seeds (sesame seeds, pumpkin seeds, linseed, sunflower seeds)

Mix all the ingredients together and serve.

OAT MUESLI WITH BERRIES

SERVES 4

4 tablespoons rolled oats
1 tablespoon oat germ and bran
100ml (4 fl oz) warmed soya milk
150g (5 oz) plain yoghurt
2 tablespoons honey
2 tablespoons lemon juice
1 red apple and 1 green apple, washed, cored and grated, but not peeled
4 tablespoons chopped hazelnuts
2 tablespoons blueberries or blackcurrants
4 sprigs of mint
Soak the rolled oats, oat germ and bran in soya milk in a bowl for at least two hours.

Stir in the yoghurt, honey and lemon juice, then add the apples and hazelnuts, followed by the berries just before serving. Garnish each portion with a sprig of mint and a few whole berries.

SUPER OATS

SERVES 1

25g (1 oz) oat flakes
1 tablespoon wheatgerm
100ml (4 fl oz) soya milk *or* rice milk *or* oat milk
1 tablespoon mixed ground seeds (sesame seeds, pumpkin seeds, linseed, sunflower seeds)
1 banana, peeled and sliced
1 apple, washed and chopped

Mix the oat flakes, wheatgerm and milk together. Add the seeds, banana and apple and serve.

Lunch

WINTER WARMER SOUP

Here's a wonderfully warming and easy-to-make meal in itself.

SERVES 4

1 tablespoon olive oil
1 medium onion, peeled and chopped
2 cloves garlic, peeled and crushed
700g (1½ lb) chopped fresh seasonal vegetables (e.g. potatoes, swede, celeriac, leeks, celery, carrots, broccoli, cabbage)
1 × 400g (14 oz) tin tomatoes
1 teaspoon vegetable stock concentrate e.g. Vecon

Heat the olive oil in a saucepan and briefly sauté the onion and garlic. Add the vegetables, tomatoes, enough water to cover and the vegetable stock. Simmer until the vegetables are cooked.

This soup can be liquidised or left as it is. Use potatoes in moderation if you don't want a particularly thick soup. Add lentils for a thicker, more filling version. For vegetable stew, use less water and don't liquidise.

CARROT SOUP IN THE RAW

Ever had a hot, raw soup? This soup is made cold and then heated gently, which keeps all the vitamin and mineral content intact. It's also full of fibre. Be careful not to overheat it.

SERVES 4

450g (1 lb) organic carrots, washed and cut into chunks
75g (3 oz) ground almonds
300ml (½ pint) soya milk
1 teaspoon vegetable stock concentrate e.g. Vecon
1 teaspoon dried mixed herbs

Place the carrots in a food processor and blend to a purée. Add the other ingredients and process until well combined. Warm very gently in a pan.

RAINBOW ROOT SALAD

This colourful combination of carrots, cabbage, parsnip and beetroot is more filling than you may think. Go easy on the beetroot and parsnips, as their strong taste can overpower the carrots.

SERVES 4

3 medium organic carrots, washed and grated
¼ red cabbage, washed and grated
1 small organic parsnip, washed and grated
1 beetroot, peeled and grated
2 tablespoons Essential Balance Oil (see page 193)
1 teaspoon Dijon mustard
2 cloves garlic, peeled and crushed
Lemon juice
Finely chopped parsley

Mix together all the vegetables in a large salad bowl. Mix the oil, mustard, garlic and lemon juice to taste, in a cup or jug. Pour over the vegetables and toss well. Sprinkle the parsley over the top.

RECOVERY SOUP
This soup is also blended raw, then heated to serve. You can experiment with the same principle to invent other instant, high-energy soups.

SERVES 1

2 organic carrots, washed and cut into chunks
3 heads broccoli, washed and broken into florets
1 bunch watercress, washed
75g (3 oz) tofu
100ml (4 fl oz) soya milk
2 teaspoons Vecon *or* Bouillon vegetable concentrate
tomato paste, spices *or* herbs to taste

Blend all the ingredients together in a food processor. Serve hot or cold, with oat cakes.

CARROT AND SWEET POTATO SOUP
Sweet potatoes are rich in carotenoids and vitamin E. This simple soup takes only a short time to prepare and tastes delicious. An alternative to sweet potato is butternut squash.

SERVES 2

4 medium sweet potatoes peeled and chopped into small pieces
4 large organic carrots, washed and chopped into small pieces
⅓ × 400ml (14 fl oz) can coconut milk
1 clove garlic, peeled and crushed
black pepper

Boil the sweet potatoes and carrots until soft in just enough water to cover. Purée in a blender, mouli, or food processor, then add the coconut milk, garlic and black pepper to taste.

Mid-afternoon snack

WATERMELON PROTECTION

The flesh of watermelon is rich in beta-carotene and vitamin C. The seeds are a great source of essential fats, vitamin E, zinc and selenium. If you blend the seeds with the flesh, the husk (the black part) of the seed sinks to the bottom and the seeds blend with the flesh to make an incredibly immune-boosting fruit drink. This is ideal during an infection as it provides enough glucose for energy, some protein from the seeds and plenty of immune-boosting nutrients. It also provides excellent protection against pollution if visiting a heavily polluted city.

BERRY JUICE COCKTAIL

There's an ever-increasing variety of fruit and berry juices available. Particularly good are loganberries, blueberries and blackcurrants. See what's available in your local healthfood store. Pick pure juices with no added sugar. These are nectar for the immune system, with plenty of vitamin C and anthocyans. They are often best diluted half and half with water to dilute the natural fruit sugars. Alternatively, make your own:

300ml (½ pint) apple juice
350g (12 oz) mixed berries (e.g. blueberries, blackberries, strawberries)

Put into a blender and whiz up.

Dinner

THAI-STYLE BUCKWHEAT NOODLES WITH SHIITAKE MUSHROOMS

Buckwheat is a wheat-free food with a good protein content. Most buckwheat noodles also contain wheat and these are easier to cook than pure buckwheat noodles, which fall apart if cooked too long. They are best boiled for five minutes, drained, then boiled again.

SERVES 2

1 tablespoon olive oil

2 cloves garlic, peeled and chopped

100g (4 oz) shiitake mushrooms (if you can't get fresh, use dried and soak them)

2 organic carrots, washed and thinly sliced lengthwise into 5cm (3 inch) lengths

100g (4 oz) broccoli, washed and broken into florets

100g (4 oz) marinated tofu pieces

1 teaspoon Thai spices plus 2 tablespoons coconut milk *or* 1 tablespoon soy sauce

200g (7 oz) buckwheat noodles

Heat the olive oil in a wok or deep frying pan. Sauté the garlic for 3 minutes, then add the mushrooms and toss briefly before adding the rest of the vegetables, tofu, spices and coconut milk and enough water for the ingredients to 'steam-fry'. Cover and turn down the heat until the vegetables are cooked but crunchy. Serve over a nest of cooked buckwheat noodles.

SALMON WITH MASHED SWEET POTATO AND BRUSSELS SPROUTS IN A HUMMUS AND MUSHROOM SAUCE

SERVES 2

2 pieces salmon fillet *or* 2 salmon steaks

2 teaspoons vegetable stock concentrate e.g. Vecon (optional)

2 large sweet potatoes, peeled and cut into chunks

black pepper

225g (8 oz) Brussels sprouts, washed and trimmed

225g (8 oz) shiitake mushrooms

1 tablespoon olive oil

100g (4 oz) hummus

Wash the salmon and pat dry with kitchen paper. Dilute the vegetable stock concentrate in 600ml (1 pint) boiling water in a large saucepan. Leave to cool until just warm. Place the salmon in the stock and bring gently up to a simmer. Poach for a few minutes. Alternatively, grill the salmon under a moderate heat, for a few minutes on each side, until just cooked.

Meanwhile, boil and mash the sweet potatoes, adding black pepper to taste. Boil or steam the Brussels sprouts for 5 minutes. Sauté the mushrooms in the oil for 2 minutes, then add a little water, cover and turn the heat down. Let them cook for 5 minutes until tender and juicy. Purée the mushrooms and add the hummus.

Arrange the salmon, mashed sweet potatoes and Brussels sprouts on a plate, pour the sauce over the fish and serve.

FISH STEW WITH ARTICHOKES AND OYSTER MUSHROOMS

SERVES 4

450g (1 lb) thick-cut, skinless salmon fillet

450g (1 lb) thick-cut mackerel fillet

black pepper

3 tablespoons cornflour

2 tablespoons olive oil

2 onions, peeled and cut into 8 wedges, retaining the root to hold the layers together

2 cloves garlic, peeled and chopped

300ml (½ pint) white wine

175ml (6 fl oz) fish stock

225g (8 oz) oyster mushrooms

1 bay leaf

2 tablespoons chopped fresh parsley

12 artichoke hearts in oil

1 lemon

2 tablespoons chopped fresh basil

Cut the fish up into bite-size chunks, removing any bones. Season with black pepper and dust with cornflour. Heat the olive oil in a deep pan. Add the chunks of fish and cook until sealed all over. Remove the fish with a slotted spoon and set aside.

Add the onions to the pan and cook until softened. Add the garlic and cook for 2 minutes. Stir in the wine and stock, the mushrooms, bayleaf and parsley. Bring to the boil and simmer for 5 minutes. (Boiling evaporates the alcohol content of the wine.)

Drain and halve the artichoke hearts. Cut the lemon into thin slices. Add the fish and artichokes to the sauce, then lay the lemon slices on top. Cover and cook for 10–15 minutes. Stir in the chopped basil. Serve immediately with brown rice.

(These and many more are to be found in the *Optimum Nutrition Cookbook*, published September 1999.)

CHAPTER 24

SUPPLEMENTARY BENEFIT

In addition to eating an immune-boosting anti-cancer diet, there's definite value in taking supplements of certain vitamins, minerals and herbs. The ideal intake depends very much on your particular needs – a consequence of genetic factors, your diet, lifestyle and environment. The 'basic' recommendations given below are therefore only a general guide for people wanting to minimise their risk of getting cancer and many other nutrition-related diseases. They are your 'insurance policy'.

In practical terms, the easiest way to achieve these levels is to supplement:

- A good all-round multivitamin and mineral

- Vitamin C (with bioflavonoids)

- An antioxidant complex (for A, C, E, zinc and selenium, plus other anti-oxidant phytonutrients such as anthocyanidins with glutathione)

Although the value of giving micronutrients to cancer patients is not generally acknowledged by the medical establishment, there is now substantial evidence for its effectiveness. The levels needed for these nutrients to exert their most positive effect far exceed the amounts needed for basic prevention. Such levels are given in the table below under 'maximum nutritional support'. They do not cover requirements during chemotherapy, radiation or surgery. Nutritional needs under these circumstances are discussed in Chapter 26.

A further argument for micronutrient supplementation is that many cancer patients suffer from malabsorption and may not be getting the micronutrients they need from their food, even if their diet is good. In any event, if you have been diagnosed with cancer you should not undertake an extensive nutritional strategy on your own. Seek the guidance of a clinical nutritionist who can work with your doctor to devise the most appropriate strategy for you. Just because a substance is 'natural' it doesn't mean it is never harmful. Very high doses of nutrients can have adverse effects and this is why you need a clinical nutritionist to advise you and run tests to find out what you need.

Ideal supplementary nutrient intake to protect against cancer

Nutrient	Basic Prevention	Maximum Nutritional Support
Vitamins		
Vitamin A	20,000iu	35,000iu
as retinol	7500iu	18,500iu*
as beta-carotene	12,500iu (20mg)	16,500iu (30mg)
Vitamin C	2000mg	10,000mg
Vitamin D	400iu	
Vitamin E	150mg (200iu)	400mg (600iu)
B1 (Thiamine)	25mg	
B2 (Riboflavin)	25mg	
B3 (Niacin)	25mg	100mg
B5 (Pantothenic acid)	25mg	50–100mg
B6 (Pyridoxine)	25mg	50–100mg

Nutrient	Basic Prevention	Maximum Nutritional Support
Vitamins – *contd*		
B12	10mcg	20mcg
Folic acid	100mcg	400mcg
Biotin	50mcg	
Minerals		
Calcium	350mg	800mg
Magnesium	200mg	500mg
Zinc	15mg	25mg
Iron	10mg	
Manganese	5mg	10mg
Chromium	50mcg	100mcg
Selenium	100mcg	200mcg
Other Nutrients		
Glutamine	1000mg	5000mg
Co-Q10	30mg	90mg
Reduced glutathione**	50mg	300mg
Anthocyanidins	20mg	50mg
Bioflavonoids	100	300mg
Herbs		
Essiac combination		as instructed
Cat's claw		1000–2000mg (1–2 cups)
Echinacea		1000–2000mg (30–60 drops)
Aloe vera		as instructed
Mushrooms (Ganoderma, etc.)		1500mg

Optional extras include: milk thistle, curcumin, bromelain, astragalus and garlic, which are all available as supplements. There are many different sources of bioflavonoids and anthocyanidins such as pycnogenol, quercitin and grape seed extract. Supplements containing a complex of anthocyanidins and bioflavonoids are becoming widely available. Also of interest for hormone-related cancers are extracts from soya rich in genistein, daidzein and other isoflavonoids.

* Do not take this amount of retinol, the non-vegetable form of vitamin A, if you are pregnant or likely to conceive.

** Glutathione must be enteric-coated to prevent degradation in the stomach. It must also be combined with anthocyans which recycle glutathione, making it much more powerful.

CHAPTER 25

LIFESTYLE CHANGES

The combination of changing your diet, taking protective nutritional supplements and making a few lifestyle changes designed to reduce your exposure to carcinogens is likely to reduce your overall risk of developing cancer by at least 50 per cent, if not 90 per cent. In real terms this means adding 10–20 years to your life (as well as adding life to your years). Your greatest chance of reducing risk is by starting early – it is never too soon for prevention.

These are the top ten lifestyle tips for reducing your exposure to potential carcinogens. Some are relatively easy to put into effect. Others, such as cutting down your exposure to exhaust fumes, depend on where you choose to live and work, and how you get from home to work and vice versa. Such factors should be part of your long-term plan. Your health is your greatest asset. It is worth protecting.

- Don't smoke and minimise the time you spend in smoky environments.

- Minimise the time you spend in traffic jams, breathing in exhaust fumes, and, if possible, live in a less polluted area.

- Minimise your exposure to very strong sun and use a good sunscreen, especially if you have fair hair, light eyes and many moles. Don't combine alcohol and strong sunlight.

- Use natural alternatives to drugs whenever possible. Don't have oestrogen- or progestin-containing HRT and only have an X-ray if it is absolutely essential.

- If you use a mobile phone, use it infrequently and use an ear-phone attachment.

- Don't heat food in plastic, and reduce the amount of drinks and fatty foods you buy that are packaged in direct contact with soft plastics.

- Switch to natural detergents and check that your bathroom and household products don't contain known carcinogens.

- Don't use pesticides in your garden or on your indoor pot plants.

- Control the level of stress in your life. Prolonged stress depletes your immune strength.

- Get enough sleep. It is a vital nutrient for the immune system.

CHAPTER 26

MAXIMISING RECOVERY

If you have been diagnosed with cancer you will probably have been offered one or more of three treatments: surgery, chemotherapy or radiotherapy. There are advantages and disadvantages to each of these treatments, the disadvantages of which can often be counteracted by specific nutritional strategies.

The purpose of this chapter is to give you information about different forms of cancer treatment and how optimum nutrition can improve your body's response to them. You should carefully consider what course of action to take, in consultation with both your doctor and a clinical nutritionist who can advise you on the most appropriate nutritional support.

SURGERY

Surgery is naturally traumatic to the body and most effective when a tumour is interfering with the body's ability to function. Surgery leaves behind cancer cells in 25–60 per cent of cancer patients, allowing malignant growth to re-occur, as numerous studies have shown. It is not a cure as such, since the tumour is the symptom rather than the cause of the underlying disease process. Before and after surgery it is wise to increase your intake of vitamin A, C, E, zinc and glutamine which help the body to heal.

RADIOTHERAPY

Radiation is used to slow down certain cancers but rarely provides a cure. Some damage will also occur to healthy cells and organ tissue. Like chemotherapy, radiation is a carcinogen itself and greatly weakens the immune system. Nutritional support during radiation is important, especially with anti-oxidant nutrients (vitamins A, C and E and selenium) glutathione.

CHEMOTHERAPY

Chemotherapy is the administration of drugs that are toxic to cancer cells. The trouble is that many of these drugs also harm healthy cells and are carcinogens in their own right. This applies both to powerful chemotherapeutic agents and mild ones such as Tamoxifen. As ever, researchers are trying to develop more specifically targeted chemotherapeutic drugs that won't damage healthy cells.

Despite being the most commonly prescribed breast cancer drug, Tamoxifen is a double-edged sword. Chemically related to DES (a drug that caused cancer in people exposed to it during foetal development), it is a weakly oestrogenic chemical which acts as an oestrogen blocker, much like plant oestrogens in soya. It is only likely to be effective in post-menopausal women who have oestrogen-sensitive breast cancer and even then the protective effects wear off after five years. While some studies have shown that it reduced their chances of developing cancer in the other breast by 30 to 50 per cent,[1] others show marginal benefit. A review of a number of studies involving 30,000 breast cancer patients, published in *The Lancet* medical journal, found only a 3.5 per cent difference in survival after five or six years in those taking the drug compared to those taking a placebo.[2]

However, there is a dark side to Tamoxifen. While it might

slightly reduce the risk of breast cancer, it has repeatedly been shown to increase the risk of liver cancer and double the risk of endometrial cancer[3], as well as carrying side effects ranging from eye damage and risk of blood clots to menopausal symptoms. As such, it is a known carcinogen. Despite all this, Tamoxifen is now being licensed to be given to women without breast cancer on the grounds that it will prevent it. This is lunacy, in the light of the known disadvantages of this drug and the overwhelming evidence on non-toxic dietary strategies that provide significantly more protection.

NUTRITIONAL SUPPORT FOR CHEMOTHERAPY AND RADIOTHERAPY

For people receiving chemotherapy or radiotherapy it is useful to know that numerous clinical studies have shown that making dietary and lifestyle changes can help improve general well-being, increase life expectancy and help reduce the effects of the therapies. Factors involved include reducing fat intake, eating more vegetables, taking vitamin and mineral supplements, minimising exposure to pollution and others.[4] Although many people are advised not to take vitamin or mineral supplements during chemotherapy or radiotherapy, several studies have shown that anti-oxidants can not only protect against the toxicity of the drugs and radiation but can also enhance their cancer-killing effects[5]. Supplementing vitamin B6 can also prevent nausea and vomiting caused by radiotherapy.

One common chemotherapeutic agent, Adriamycin, has the unfortunate side-effect of inducing heart problems. Since it is known to deplete levels of Co-Q – which is essential for heart function – a group of patients were given 100mg of Co-Q daily during chemotherapy and compared to other patients given chemotherapy alone. Those on Co-Q did not experience the increase in cardiac problems that occurred in the group not supplementing Co-Q[6].

Another nutrient worth supplementing during chemotherapy is bromelain, a protein-digesting enzyme found in pineapple. In one study conducted in Germany giving bromelain alongside chemotherapy produced significant tumour regression. The researchers found that up to 2g of bromelain a day was needed for optimal effects.[7]

In addition to the nutrients recommended in Chapter 24, the amino acid glutamine can greatly help recovery after surgery and during chemotherapy. Glutamine is the primary nutrient for the lining of the small intestine and may be useful for healing a variety of inflammatory gut conditions. It is also a precursor for the key anti-oxidant glutathione. Patients receiving chemotherapy frequently suffer from nausea, vomiting and diarrhoea, probably because the chemotherapy attacks and destroys the fast-growing intestinal cells. In one study, 11 patients undergoing chemotherapy for acute leukaemia received 6g of oral glutamine three times a day for three days prior to therapy, and then for 11 to 39 days afterwards. Compared to the 22 subjects in the control group, the glutamine group experienced less severe diarrhoea, for a significantly shorter period of time.[8]

Other studies have shown that glutamine speeds up recovery from chemotherapy and reduces the incidence of infection,[9] a common occurrence following these powerful drugs. Likewise, animal studies have shown that chemotherapy is more effective when glutamine is also given.[10] It also reduces injury from radiation. However, as glutamine can enhance the effectiveness of chemotherapy, it should, in such a situation, only be used under medical supervision.

NATURAL CANCER STRATEGIES

Should you choose to pursue an aggressive nutritional approach to cancer, this is best done with the guidance of a clinical nutritionist. On the basis of a complete assessment of your nutritional needs they can work out the most appropriate strategy for you. This is likely to include the following:

- **Blood and urine tests** to determine your current health status. This can include assessing your current risk from DNA assays, anti-oxidant status and assessing your detoxification potential. These advanced tests help to pinpoint the best course of action.

- **A detoxifying diet**, aimed at giving your body maximum nutrients with minimum ingestion of toxic substances.

- **A nutritional supplement programme**, with high levels of anti-oxidants and key nutrients known to boost your immune system and stack the odds in your favour. This is likely to include large amounts of vitamins A and C, and selenium, as well as glutathione and anthocyanidins.

- **Natural anti-cancer agents**, depending on your type of cancer. For hormone-related cancers this may involve phyto-oestrogens such as genistein and daidzein from soya. There are a number of other anti-cancer agents that they can advise you about.

- **Support** is an important part of the process and there are a number of support groups for people with cancer and for those who choose non-conventional treatments.

- **Education** is also a vital ally. The more you know, the greater your ability to make informed choices.

To find a clinical nutritionist in your area, see Useful Addresses. Some have more experience of working with people with cancer so it's worth asking around before making your choice. Pursuing a nutritional strategy is *not* an alternative to medical treatment. In fact, the two together may produce the best outcome.

That's the opinion of cancer specialist Dr Keith Block, director of the Integrative Cancer Care Center in Evanston, Illinois. Block and his colleagues combine cautious amounts of chemotherapy, radiotherapy and surgery with generous amounts of supplements, diet advice and psychological support. In the same way, your clinical nutritionist and doctor and whomever else you choose to employ should be viewed as members of a team whose purpose is to provide you with the best possible strategy for restoring health.

The next section of this book identifies which dietary factors and nutritional supplements have the most prevention power for each type of cancer.

PART 6

A–Z OF NUTRITIONAL HEALING

BREAST CANCER

Breast cancer is the most prevalent cancer among women, and it can also occur in men. Around 80 per cent of breast cancers are termed oestrogen-receptor positive. There is a high likelihood that hormone-disrupting chemicals play a part in such cancers (see Chapters 3 and 15). Diets high in meat and saturated fat may mean more exposure to such chemicals which can be stored in fat tissue.

Associated risk factors: Oral contraceptive use, hormone replacement therapy containing oestrogens or synthetic progestins, high body fat percentage and waist-to-hip ratio, rapid early development and early menstruation, high-fat diet, high saturated fat and excess calorie intake, alcohol consumption above one or two drinks a day, smoking, high meat consumption, low intake of fruit and vegetables, exposure to pesticides, hormone-disrupting chemicals, radiation (including mammograms), presence of the genes (BRCA1 and 2-oncogenes), and low dietary fibre.

Prevention: Follow the general advice in Part 5. Particularly important nutrients are vitamins D and E, and the minerals selenium and calcium. The lowest risk diet is vegan (no meat, no dairy). Eat organic wherever possible. Fish, especially mackerel, herring, tuna and salmon which are rich in Omega-3 fats, lower risk. Flax seeds and their oil are the best vegetarian source of Omega-3 fats. Regular consumption of soya (such as tofu or soya milk) also lowers risk. Tomatoes, rich in lycopene, are also recommended.

Nutritional support: Recommended are maximum support levels (see page 155) of vitamin C, E and calcium. Consider a supplemental source of genistein and daidzein, the protective factors found in soya.

CERVICAL CANCER

Cervical cancer can now be diagnosed early with Pap smears. The pre-invasive form is almost always curable and early diagnosis has led to a 70 per cent reduction in death rate.

Associated risk factors: Infection with human papillomavirus (HPV) – many sexual partners increase risk of this, oral contraceptives, smoking, low carotenoids, low vitamin C, low intake of fruit and vegetables providing carotenoids and vitamin C, exposure to hormone-disrupting chemicals.

Prevention: Follow the general advice in Part 5. Particularly important nutrients are vitamins D and E, and the minerals selenium and calcium. The lowest risk diet is vegan (no meat, no dairy). Eat organic wherever possible. Regular consumption of soya (such as tofu or soya milk) is also likely to lower risk.

Nutritional support: Pre-malignant changes in cervical cells, called cervical dysplasia, respond well to vitamin C and folic acid. These are recommended at maximum support levels (see page 155), together with anti-oxidant vitamins: A, beta-carotene and E.

COLORECTAL CANCER

Cancers of the colon or rectum are some of the most common cancers, particularly in the Western world. They are strongly linked to diet and there is little doubt that dietary carcinogens, caused by putrefying food, and created by micro-organisms in an unhealthy gut, play a big part. A high-fibre diet shortens the time food takes to pass through the digestive tract and reduces carcinogen exposure.

Associated risk factors: High-fat (especially saturated fat) diet, high meat consumption (especially grilled, barbecued or burnt meat), low fibre intake, history of polyps, smoking, excess alcohol, lack of exercise, lack of vegetables, high calories, prolonged stress.

Prevention: Follow the general advice in Part 5. Particularly important nutrients are beta-carotene, vitamin C, folic acid, vitamin D, calcium and selenium. Diet, however, is the major prevention factor. Regular garlic consumption reduces risk, as does live yoghurt which provides beneficial bacteria to improve intestinal health.

Nutritional support: Recommended are maximum support levels (see page 155) of beta-carotene, vitamin C, folic acid, vitamin D, calcium and selenium, and a strict dietary regime.

ENDOMETRIAL (UTERINE) CANCER

The endometrium is the lining of the womb (the uterus). Endometrial cancer is very much on the increase – it is a hormone-sensitive cancer that shares many risk factors with breast cancer. There is a high likelihood that hormone-disrupting chemicals play a part in such cancers (see Chapters 3 and 15).

Associated risk factors: Obesity, high intake of saturated and animal fats, low intake of fruit and vegetables high in carotenoids and vitamin C, exposure to hormone-disrupting chemicals, oral contraceptive use, and HRT containing oestrogen or synthetic progestins, Tamoxifen.

Prevention: Follow the general advice in Part 5. Particularly important nutrients are vitamins D and E, and the minerals selenium and calcium. The lowest risk diet is vegan (no meat, no dairy). Eat organic wherever possible. Fish, especially mackerel, herring, tuna and salmon which are rich in Omega-3 fats, lower risk. Flax seeds and their oil are the best vegetarian source of Omega-3 fats. Regular consumption of soya (such as tofu or soya milk) also lowers risk. Tomatoes, rich in lycopene, are also recommended.

Nutritional support: Recommended are maximum support levels (see page 155) of vitamin C, E and calcium. Consider a supplemental source of genistein and daidzein, the protective factors found in soya.

KIDNEY AND BLADDER

The kidneys filter the blood, removing toxic material and passing it on to the bladder. It is very likely that a poor diet, plus exposure to toxins and carcinogens, increases the risk of either of these types of cancer. Improving detoxification potential may reduce risk (see Chapter 6).

Associated risk factors: Low intake of fruit and vegetables, high intake of dairy produce, and obesity.

Prevention: Follow the general advice in Part 5. Particularly important nutrients are all anti-oxidants, especially selenium in the case of bladder cancer.

Nutritional support: Recommended are maximum support levels (see page 155) of vitamins A, C and E, beta-carotene and selenium.

LIVER

The liver is the primary organ of detoxification and liver cancer is highly indicative of over-exposure to and/or an inability to detoxify carcinogens. Improving your detoxification potential may reduce risk (see Chapter 6).

Associated risk factors: Alcohol, Tamoxifen, and possibly long-term use of other prescribed medical and recreational drugs used in excess.

Prevention: Follow the general advice in Part 5. Particularly important nutrients are all anti-oxidants, including selenium, and cruciferous vegetables such as broccoli, cauliflower, kale, cabbage and Brussels sprouts.

Nutritional Support: Recommended are maximum support levels (see page 155) of vitamins A, C and E, beta-carotene and selenium, which help the liver detoxify. The herb milk thistle may also be beneficial. Clinical nutritionists can test which pathways in the liver are most overloaded and devise a nutritional strategy to ease the load.

LUNG

Lung cancer is the most prevalent cancer in men and is also exceedingly common in women. While smoking is a major factor, diet plays an important role too. In countries where smoking is on the decrease, so too is lung cancer (see Chapter 16).

Associated risk factors: Smoking, alcohol, excess fat and saturated fat, lack of fruit and vegetables especially carotenoids, high pollution or diesel fuel or radon exposure.

Prevention: Follow the general advice in Part 5. Particularly important nutrients are all anti-oxidants, including selenium and beta-carotene. Eat a carrot every day and don't smoke.

Nutritional support: Recommended are maximum support levels (see page 155) of vitamins A, C and E, beta-carotene and selenium.

LYMPHOMA (NON-HODGKIN'S) AND LEUKAEMIA

Non-Hodgkin's lymphoma and leukemia are less common cancers, although the incidence of non-Hodgkin's lymphoma is on the increase.

Associated risk factors: Not much is known about the risk factors for these cancers. However, pesticide exposure is a risk factor for both and radiation is a risk factor for leukaemia.

Prevention: Follow the general advice in Part 5. Probably important are all anti-oxidants, including selenium and beta-carotene which help to detoxify the body. Eating a diet high in organic fruit and vegetables, especially cruciferous vegetables such as broccoli, cauliflower, kale, cabbage and Brussels sprouts and low in red meat and dairy, may decrease toxic load and risk.

Nutritional support: Recommended are maximum support levels (see page 155) of vitamins A, C and E, beta-carotene and selenium.

MOUTH, THROAT AND OESOPHAGUS

The location of these cancers is strongly suggestive of ingested or inhaled carcinogens.

Associated risk factors: Alcohol, smoking, lack of fruit and vegetables, high intake of maté tea, or very hot drinks. The combination of smoking and drinking increases risk of oesophageal cancer.

Prevention: Follow the general advice in Part 5. Probably important are the anti-oxidants vitamin C, vitamin A, and selenium, plus a diet high in fruit and vegetables and low in alcohol. Avoid smoking and very hot drinks.

Nutritional support: Recommended are Maximum Support Levels (see page 155) of vitamins A and C, plus selenium.

OVARIAN CANCER

Ovarian cancer is rather uncommon and its prevalence is not increasing significantly. Problems with ovulation, coupled with exposure to hormone-disrupting chemicals, may possibly play a part. Little is known at this stage, although there is good logic to follow the recommendations for breast cancer.

Associated risk factors: Exposure to hormone-disrupting chemicals, oral contraceptive use, and HRT containing oestrogen or synthetic progestins.

Prevention: Probably the same as for breast cancer, namely to follow the general advice in Part 5. Important nutrients may be vitamins D and E, and the minerals selenium and calcium. The lowest risk diet is vegan (no meat, no dairy). Eat organic wherever possible. Fish, especially mackerel, herring, tuna and salmon which are rich in Omega-3 fats, lower risk. Flax seeds and their oil are the best vegetarian source of Omega-3 fats. Regular consumption of soya (such as tofu or soya milk) also lowers risk. Tomatoes, rich in lycopene, are also recommended.

Nutritional support: Recommended are maximum support levels (see page 155) of vitamins C and E and calcium. Consider a supplemental source of genistein and daidzein, the protective factors found in soya.

PANCREAS

The pancreas produces enzymes to digest foods, as well as hormones. This less common type of cancer interferes with digestion, often impeding optimal nutrition.

Associated risk factors: Low intakes of fruit and vegetables, low intake of fibre, high consumption of meat, smoking, and possibly excessive coffee consumption, although not all studies agree.

Prevention: Follow the general advice in Part 5. Probably important are the anti-oxidants vitamin C, vitamin A, and selenium, plus a diet high in fruit and vegetables and low in meat and alcohol. Avoid smoking and excessive coffee consumption.

Nutritional support: Recommended are maximum support levels (see page 155) of the anti-oxidants: vitamins A, C and E and selenium. Digestive enzymes and specially prepared food, soups and juices may be necessary to assist digestion and absorption of nutrients.

PROSTATE

This is the most rapidly increasing cancer in men; it is predicted to become the most common within 20 years, possibly affecting as many as one in four men at some point during their life. Its causes and nutritional approach are very similar to breast cancer. There is a high likelihood that hormone-disrupting chemicals play a part in these (see Chapters 3 and 15).

Associated risk factors: High-fat and high saturated fat diet, regular consumption of dairy products and meat, low fibre intake, obesity, smoking, high cadmium levels, exposure to hormone-disrupting chemicals and pesticides, high levels of testosterone.

Prevention: Follow the general advice in Part 5. Particularly important nutrients are vitamins A and E and beta-carotene and the minerals selenium and zinc. The lowest risk diet is vegan (no meat, no dairy). Eat organic wherever possible. Fish, especially mackerel, herring, tuna and salmon which are rich in Omega-3 fats, lower risk. Flax seeds and their oil are the best vegetarian source of Omega-3 fats. Regular consumption of soya (such as tofu or soya milk) also lowers risk. Tomatoes, rich in lycopene, are also recommended.

Nutritional support: Recommended are maximum support levels (see page 155) of vitamins A and E and beta-carotene and the minerals selenium and zinc. Consider a supplemental source of genistein and daidzein, the protective factors found in soya and possibly the herb Saw palmetto, which helps benign prostatic hyperplasia.

SKIN

There are two main kinds of skin cancer – basal or squamous cell carcinoma and melanoma. Skin carcinoma is both common and relatively easy to treat. Melanoma is rare and highly malignant, and hence represents more of a risk. Excessive exposure to strong sunlight is the main risk factor (see Chapter 14).

Associated risk factors: Excessive exposure to ultraviolet light, especially in fair-skinned people with red or blonde hair and those with a lot of moles; high dairy consumption.

Prevention: Follow the general advice in Part 5, especially avoiding exposure to strong sunlight without wearing an appropriate sunblock. Particularly important nutrients are vitamin E and beta-carotene, although all anti-oxidants help to protect against skin damage.

Nutritional support: Recommended are maximum support levels (see page 155) of the anti-oxidants vitamins A, C and E, beta-carotene and selenium.

STOMACH

Stomach cancer is very strongly linked to dietary carcinogens. It can be prevented both by avoiding high-risk foods and having a good intake of nutrients which can disarm carcinogens in food.

Associated risk factors: Salt and salted foods; grilled, fried, barbecued or burnt meat; lack of refrigeration introducing pathogens; low intake of fresh fruit and vegetables.

Prevention: Follow the general advice in Part 5. Particularly important nutrients are the antioxidants beta-carotene, vitamin C and selenium. Regular garlic consumption is also protective.

Nutritional support: Recommended are maximum support levels (see page 155) of the antioxidant vitamins A, C and E, beta-carotene and selenium.

TESTICULAR CANCER

Testicular cancer is the most common type of cancer in men under 35. Although it is still quite rare, with just over 1500 new cases a year in the UK, it is a matter for concern that the incidence has doubled in the last 20 years. It is, however, the most curable of all cancers – over 90% of sufferers make a complete recovery. Early detection is crucial, so men are encouraged to check their testes monthly for any changes such as lumps, swelling or hardening.

Associated risk factors: Men who are born with an undescended testicle are five times more likely to develop the disease. Other risk factors are a family history of the disease, early puberty and low levels of exercise.

Prevention: Follow the general advice for minimising your cancer risk given in Part 5. Minimise your intake of meat and dairy products, eat plenty of fruit, vegetables and fibre and eat organic as much as possible. Avoid alcohol, recreational drugs and smoking and limit coffee consumption. Ensure a good intake of anti-oxidants.

Nutritional support: Maximum nutritional support given on page 151.

REFERENCES

Part 1

1 Waller, R., 'The Diseases of Civilisation', *The Ecologist*, vol 1:2 (1970).

2 East Anglian Cancer Intelligence Unit, Department of Community Medicine, University of Cambridge, *Report of Cancer Incidence and Projections*, for Macmillan Cancer Relief (June 1997).

3 Ibid.

4 Epstein, S., 'Winning the War Against Cancer? . . . Are they even fighting it?' *The Ecologist*, vol 28:2 pp 69–80 (1998).

5 Shekelle et al., *The Lancet*, vol 2, pp 186–90 (1981).

6 Epstein, S., op. cit.

7 Typescript of interview with Simon Wolff by Andrew Baron, 13 May 1993.

8 Ostrerline, A., 'Diverging trends in incidence and mortality of testicular cancer in Denmark: 1943–1982', *Cancer*, vol 53, pp 501–5 (1986).
East Anglian Cancer Intelligence Unit, op. cit.

9 National Cancer Institute, 'Bioassay of chloradane for possible carcinogenicity', Carcinogenesis Technical Report Series No. 8 (1977).

10 Scribner, J.D. and Mottet, N.D., 'DDT acceleration of mammary gland tumors induced in the male Sprague-Dawley rat by 2-acetamidophenanthrene', *Carcinogenesis*, vol 2, pp 1235–9 (1981).

11 Westin, J.B. and Richter, E., 'The Israeli breast-cancer anomaly', *Ann NY Acad Sci*, vol 609, pp 269–79 (1990).

12 Wasserman, M. et al., 'Organochlorine compounds in neoplastic

and adjacent apparently normal breast tissue', *Bull Environ Contam Toxicol*, vol 15, pp 478–84 (1976).

13 Soto, A. et al., 'P-nonylphenol: and estrogenic xenobiotic released from "modified" polystyrene', *Environmental Health Perspectives*, vol 92, pp 167–73 (1991).

14 Chang et al., *Fertility and Sterility*, 63(4) (1995).

15 Herbst, A. et al., *N Engl J Med*, vol 284, pp 878–81 (1971).

16 Gill, W. et al., 'Effects on human males of in utero exposure to exogenous sex hormones'.
Miri, T. and Nagasawa, H. (eds) *Toxicity of Hormones in Perinatal Life*, CRC Press (1988).

17 Bergkvist, L. et al., 'The risk of breast cancer after estrogen and estrogen-progestin replacement', *N Eng J Med*, vol 32, pp 293–7 (1989).

18 Colditz, G. et al., 'The use of estrogen and progestins and the risk of breast cancer in postmenopausal women', *N Engl J Med*, vol 332, pp 1589–93 (1995).

19 Collaborative Group on Hormonal Factors in Breast Cancer, 'Breast cancer and hormone replacement therapy: collaborative reanalysis of data from 51 epidemiological studies of 52,705 woman with breast cancer and 108,411 women without breast cancer', *Lancet*, vol 350, pp 1047–59 (1997).

20 Rodriguez, C. et al., 'Estrogen replacement therapy and fatal ovarian cancer', *Am J Epidemiology*, vol 141(9), pp 828–35 (1995).

21 Beresford, S.A. et al., 'Risk of endometrial cancer in relation to use of oestrogen combined with cyclic progestagen therapy in postmenopausal women', *Lancet*, vol 349(9050), pp 458–61 (1997).

22 Messina, M., 'The role of soy products in reducing risk of cancer', *J Natl Cancer Inst*, vol 83, pp 541–46 (1991).
Troll, W., 'Soybean diet lowers breast tumour incidence in irradiated rats', *Carcinogenesis*, vol 1, pp 469–72 (1980).

23 Barnes, S., 'Soybeans inhibit mammary tumor growth in models of breast cancer', *Mutagens and Carcinogens in Diet*, Pariza, M. (ed), Wiley, New York (1990).

24 Epstein, S., op. cit.

25 Howard, V., 'Synergistic effect of chemical mixtures: can we rely on traditional toxicology?' *The Ecologist*, vol 27(5) (1997).

26 Watson, P. et al., 'Prognosis of BRCA1 hereditary breast cancer (commentary)', *Lancet*, vol 351, pp 304–5 (1998).

27 Murphy, P. and Bra, W., 'How cancer gene testing can benefit patients', *Mol Med Today*, vol 3(4), pp 147–152 (1997).

28 Katiyar, S. et al., 'Protective effects of silymarin against photo-carcinogenes in a mouse skin model', *J Natl Cancer Inst*, vol 8(98), pp 556–66 (1997).

29 Pinner, R. et al., 'Trends in infectious diseases mortality in the United States', *JAMA*, vol 275(3), pp 189–93 (1996).

30 *The Health of Adult Britain* 1841–1994, Office of National Statistics.

31 *Daily Mail*, 15/4/97, p 11.

Part 2

1 Mann, J. et al., 'Risk of death from cancer and ischaemic heart disease in meat and non-meat-eaters', *Br Med J*, vol 308, pp 1667–70 (1994).

2 Giovannucci, E. et al., 'A prospective study of dietary fat and risk of prostate cancer', *J Natl Cancer Inst*, vol 85, pp 1571–9 (1993).

3 Cox, B.D. and Whichelow, M.J., 'Frequent consumption of red meat is not a risk factor for cancer', (letter), *BMJ*, vol 315(7114), pp 1018 (1997).

4 Lindblad, P. et al., 'Diet and risk of renal cell cancer: a population-based case-control study', *Cancer Epidemiol Biomarkers Prev*, vol 6(4), pp 215–23 (1997).

5 Peters, R.K. et al., 'Diet and colon cancer in Los Angeles County, California', *Cancer Causes Control*, vol 3(5), pp 457–73 (1992).

6 de Lorgeril, M. et al., 'Mediterranean dietary pattern in a ran-domised trial: prolonged survival and possible reduced cancer rate', *Arch Intern Med*, vol 158(11), pp 1181–1188 (1998).

7 Lindblad, P. et al., op. cit.

8 *Longevity* (November 1995).

9 *Clinical Pearls News*, vol 6(3) (1996).

10 Hirayama, T., 'A large scale cohort study on cancer risks by diet – with special reference to the risk reducing effects of green-yellow vegetables consumption', *Princess Takamatsu Symp*, vol 16, pp 41–53 (1985).

11 'Food, Nutrition and the Prevention of Cancer', World Cancer Research Fund, American Institute for Cancer Research, pp 239–42 (1997).

12 Pool-Zobel, B.L. et al., 'Consumption of vegetables reduces genetic damage in humans: first results of a human intervention trial with carotenoid-rich foods', *Carcinogenesis*, vol 18(9), pp 1847–50 (1997).

13 Goldschmidt-Clermant, R., 'Mitogenic signaling mediated by oxidants in pastransformed fibroblasts', *Science* (14/3/97).

14 Peters, R. et al., *Cancer Causes and Control*, vol 3, pp 457–73 (1992).

15 *Carcinogens*, vol 16 (1995).

16 Grubbs, C.J. et al., 'Chemoprevention of chemically-induced mammary carcinogenesis by indole-3-carbinol', *Anticancer Res*, vol 15(3), pp 709–16 (1995).
Preobrazhenshaya, M.N. et al., 'Polyfunctional indole-3-carbinol derivatives: I-(indol-3-yl) glycerols and related compounds, beta-hydroxytryptamines and ascorbigens. Chemistry and biological properties', *Farmaco*, vol 50(6), pp 369–77 (1995).

17 Adlercreutz, H. et al., 'Plasma concentrations of phyto-oestrogens in Japanese men', *Lancet*, vol 342, pp 1209–10 (1993).

18 St Clair, W.H. and St Clair, D.K., 'Effect of the Bowman-Birk protease inhibitor on the expression of oncogenes in the irradiated rat colon', *Cancer Res*, vol 51, pp 4539–43 (1991).
St Clair, W.H. et al., 'Suppression of dimethylyhydrazine-induced carcinogenesis in mice by dietary addition of the Bowman-Birk protease inhibitor', *Cancer Res*, vol 50, pp 580–86 (1990).

19 Lu, L.J. et al., 'Altered time course of urinary diadzein and genistein excretion during chronic soya diet in healthy male subjects', *Nutr Cancer*, vol 24, pp 311–23 (1995).

20 Ingram, D. et al., 'Case-control study of phyto-oestrogens and breast cancer', *Lancet*, vol 350, pp 990–94 (1997).
Messina, M. et al., 'Phyto-oestrogens and breast cancer', *Lancet*, vol 350, pp 971–72 (1997).

21 Dwyer, J. et al., 'Tofu and soy drinks contain phytoestrogens', *J Am Diet Assoc*, vol 94(7), pp 739–43 (1994).

22 Messina, M. and Messina, V., 'Increasing use of soyfoods and

their potential role in cancer prevention', *Perspectives in Practice*, vol 91(7), pp 836–40 (1991).

23 *Health Update USA* (Jan 1994) and World Cancer Research Fund Newsletter (Sept 1994).

24 Krishnaswamy, K. et al., 'Retardation of experimental tumourigenesis and reduction in DNA adducts by turmeric and curcumin', *Nutrition and Cancer*, vol 30(2), p 163 (1998).

25 Uauy-Dagach, R. and Valenzuela, A., 'Marine oils: the health benefits of *n*-3 fatty acids.' *Nutr Rev*, vol 54(11), pp S102–S108 (1996).

26 Wynder, E.L. et al., 'Breast cancer: weighing the evidence for a promoting role of dietary fat', *J Natl Cancer Inst*, vol 89(11), pp 766–75 (1997).
Hilakivi-Clarke, L. et al., 'Breast cancer risk in rats fed a diet high in n-6 polyunsaturated fatty acids during pregnancy', *J Natl Cancer Inst*, vol 88(24), pp 1821–7 (1996).

27 Simonsen, S. et al., 'Adipose tissue omega-3 and omega-6 fatty acid content and breast cancer in the EURAMIC study', *Am J Epidemiol*, vol 147, pp 342–52 (1998).

28 Gogos, C.A. et al., *Cancer* (15/1/98).

29 Boyd, N.F. et al., 'Effects at two years of a low fat, high carbohydrate diet on radiologic features of the breast: results from a randomised trial', *J Natl Cancer Inst*, vol 89(7), pp 488–96 (1977).

30 Frankel, *BMJ* (February 1998).

31 Peters, R.K. et al., op. cit.

32 Peters, R.K. et al., op. cit.

33 Royal, D. et al., 'Clinical significance of colonic fermentation', *Am J Gastroenterol*, vol 85(10), pp 1307–12 (1990).
Latella, G. and Caprilli, R., 'Metabolism of large bowel mucosa in health and disease', *Colorect Dis*, vol 6: 127–32 (1991).
Hoverstad, R., 'The normal microflora and short-chain fatty acids', Proceedings of the Fifth Bengt E. Gustafsson Symposium, Stockholm (1–4 June 1988).

34 Yuan, J.M. et al., 'Diet and breast cancer in Shanghai and Tianjin, China', *Br J Cancer*, vol 71(6), pp 1353–8 (1995).

35 De Stefani, E. et al., 'Dietary fiber and risk of breast cancer: a case-control study in Uruguay', *Nutr Cancer*, vol 28(1), pp 14–19 (1997).

36 WCRF report, op. cit (1997).

37 Smith-Warner, S.A. et al., 'Alcohol and breast cancer in women: a pooled analysis of cohort studies', *JAMA*, vol 279(7), pp 535–40 (1998).

38 Glynn, S.A. et al., 'Alcohol consumption and risk for colorectal cancer in a cohort of Finnish men', *Cancer Causes Control*, vol 7(2), pp 214–23 (1996).

39 Clifford, A. et al., 'Delayed tumor onset in transgenic mice fed an amino acid-based diet supplemented with red wine solids', *Am J Clin Nutr*, vol 64, pp 745–56 (1996).

40 WCRF report, op. cit. (1997).

41 Record, I. and Dreosti, I., 'Protection against UV-related skin damage by antioxidants', abstract from conference paper, Mount Butter International Conference on Environmental Radiation (9/12/96).

Part 3

1 Repacholi, M.H. et al., 'Lymphomas in E mu-Pim1 transgenic mice exposed to pulsed 900MHZ electromagnetic fields', *Radiation Res*, vol 145(5), pp 631–640 (1997).

2 Roy, S. et al., 'The phorbol 12-myristate 13-acetate (PMA)-induced oxidative burst in rat peritoneal neutrophils is increased by a 0.1 mT (60 Hz) magnetic field', *FEBS Lett*, vol 376(3), pp 164–6 (1995).

3 Davidson, J.A. [letter], *Med J Aust* (5 Jan 1998).

4 Repacholi, M.H., 'Low-level exposure to radiofrequency electromagnetic fields: health effects and research results', *Bioelectromagnetics*, vol 19(1), pp 1–19 (1998).

5 Gardner, M.J. et al., 'Follow-up study of children born to mothers resident in Seascale, West Cumbria (birth cohort)', *BMJ*, vol 295, pp 822–7 (1987).
Gardner, M.J. et al., 'Follow-up study of children born elsewhere but attending schools in Seascale, West Cumbria (schools cohort)', *BMJ*, vol 295, pp 819–22 (1987).

6 Darby, S. et al., 'Risk of lung cancer associated with residential radon exposure in south-west England: a case-control study', *Br J Cancer*, vol 78(3), pp 394–408 (1998).

7 Studzinski, G.P. and Moore, D.C. 'Sunlight – can it prevent as well as cause cancer?', *Cancer Res*, vol 55(18), pp 1014–22 (1995).

8 Pathak, M., 'Activtion of the melanocyte system by ultraviolet radiation and cell transformation', *Ann NY Acad Sci*, vol 453, pp 328–39 (1985).

9 Knowland, J. and McHugh, P.J., 'Characterisation of DNA damage inflicted by free radicals from a mutagenic sunscreen ingredient and its location using an in vitro genetic reversion assay', *Photochem Photobiol*, vol 66(2), pp 276–81 (1997).

10 Thornton, J., 'Chlorine, human health and the environment: the breast cancer warning', Greenpeace, Washington DC (1993).

11 *Dispatches: Breast Cancer*, Channel Four TV, (Spring 1998); Health Update USA The Lindane Legacy, Dawkins Associates, (December 1994).

12 New Zealand Total Diet Survey (1990/1991).

13 Gold, E. et al., 'Risk factors for brain tumours in children (1979).

14 Buckley, J.D. et al., 'Occupational exposures of parents of children with acute nonlymphocytaic leukemia: a report from the children's cancer study group', *Cancer Research*, vol 49, pp 4030–37 (1989).

15 Lowengart, R.A. et al., 'Childhood leukemia and parents' occupational and home exposures', *J Natl Cancer Inst*, vol 79, pp 39–46 (1987).

16 Smith, A., 'Infant exposure assessment for breast milk dioxins and furans derived from waste incineration emissions', *Risk Analysis*, vol 7(3), pp 347–53 (1987).

17 Hirayama, T., op. cit.

18 WCRF report, op. cit., pp 238–42.

19 WCRF report, op. cit.

20 Kahn, H.A., 'The Dorn study of smoking and mortality among US veterans: a report on eight and a half years of observation', in Haenszel, W. (ed), *Natl Cancer Inst Monogr*, vol 19, pp 1–125 (1966).

21 Epstein, S. op. cit.

22 Miller, G.H. et al., 'Women and lung cancer: a comparison of active and passive smokers with nonexposed nonsmokers', *Cancer Detect Prev*, vol 18(6), pp 421–30 (1994).

23 Charloux, A. et al., 'Passive smoking and bronchial cancer: a difficult relationship to establish', *Rev Pneumol Clin*, vol 62(4), pp 227–34 (1996).

24 Morabia, A. et al., 'Relation of breast cancer with passive and active exposure to tobacco smoke', *Am J Epidemiol*, vol 143(9), pp 918–28 (1996).

25 Cadbury, D., *The Feminization of Nature*, Hamish Hamilton, pp 180–3 (1997).

26 Kemeny, M. Psychological and immunological prediction of recurrence in Herpes simplex II; *Psychosomatic Med*, vol 51, pp 195–208 (1989).

27 Kiecolt-Glaser, J.K. et al., 'Distress and DNA repair in human lymphocytes', *J Behav Med*, vol 8, pp 311–19 (1985).

Part 4

1 Omenn, G. et al., 'Effects of a combination of beta carotene and vitamin A on lung cancer and cardiovascular disease', *New Engl J Med*, vol 334, pp 1150–55 (1996).

2 Podmore, I.D. et al., 'Vitamin C exhibits pro-oxidant properties', *Nature*, vol 892; 1559 (1998).

3 Basu, T. et al., 'Plasma vitamin A in patients with bronchial carcinoma', *Brit J of Cancer*, vol 33(1), pp 119–21 (1972).
Comstock, G.W. et al., 'The risk of developing lung cancer associated with anti-oxidants in the blood: ascorbic acid, carotenoids, alpha-tocopherol, selenium and total peroxyl radical absorbing capacity', *Cancer Epidemiol Biomarkers Prevention*, vol 6(11), pp 907–16 (1997).

4 Shekelle, R. et al., op. cit.

5 Bond, G. et al., 'Dietary vitamin A and lung cancer: results of a case-control study among chemical workers', *Nutrition and Cancer*, vol 9(2/3), pp 109–21 (1987).

6 Hirayama, T., 'Diet and Cancer', *Nutr Cancer*, vol 1, pp 67–8 (1979).

7 Rock, C.L. et al., 'Responsiveness of carotenoids to a high vegetable diet intervention designed to prevent breast cancer recurrence', *Cancer Epidemiological Markers*, vol 6(8), pp 617–23 (1997).

8 Dorgan, J.F. et al., 'Relationships of serum carotenoids, retinol, alpha-tocopherol and selenium with breast cancer risk: results from a prospective study in Columbia, Missouri', *Cancer Causes and Control*, vol 9, pp 89–97 (1998).

9 Stitch, H. et al., 'Response of oral leukoplakia to the administration of vitamin A', *Cancer Letters*, vol 40(1), pp 93–101 (1988).

10 Huang, L.A. et al., 'Treatment of acute promyelocytic leukemia with all-trans retinoic acid: a five-year experience', *Chin Med J*, vol 106(10), pp 43–48 (1993).

11 Lippman, S.M. et al., 'Molecular epidemiology and retinoid chemoprevention of head and neck cancer', *J Natl Cancer Inst*, vol 89(3), pp 199–211 (1997).
Lippman, S.M. and Hong, W.K., '13-cis-retinoic acid plus interferon-alpha in solid tumors: keeping the cart behind the horse', (editorial), *Ann Onco* (Netherlands), vol 5(5), pp 391–93 (1994).

12 Block, G., 'Epidemiologic evidence regarding vitamin C and cancer', *Am J Clin-Nutr*, vol 54, pp 1310S–1314S (1991).

13 Cameron, E. and Pauling, L., 'Supplemental ascorbate in the supportive treatment of cancer: prolongation of survival times in terminal human cancer', *Proc Nat Acad Sci*, vol 73(10), pp 3685–93 (1976).
Cameron, E. and Pauling, L., 'Supplemental ascorbate in the supportive treatment of cancer: Reevaluation of prolongation of survival times in terminal human cancer', *Proc Nat Acad Sci*, vol 7, pp 4538–42 (1976).
Jaffey, M. 'Vitamin C and Cancer. Examination of the value of Level trial results using broad inductive reasoning', *Med Hypothesis*, vol 8(1), pp 49–84 (1982).

14 Murata, A. and Morishige F., International Conference on Nutrition, Taijin, China 1981. Report in *Medical Tribune* (22/6/81).

15 Creagan, E.T., 'Failure of high-dose vitamin C (ascorbic acid) therapy to benefit patients with advanced cancer: a controlled trial', *New Engl J Med*, vol 301, pp 687–90 (1979).

16 Head, K.A. 'Ascorbic Acid in the prevention and treatment of cancer', *Altern Med Rev*, vol 3(3), pp 174–86 (1998).

17 Block, G., op. cit.

18 Kush, L. et al., 'Intake of vitamins A, C and E and postmenopausal breast cancer. The Iowa Women's Health Study', *Am J Epidemiol*, vol 144(2), pp 165–74 (1996).

19 Knekt, P. et al., 'Serum vitamin E and risk of cancer among Finnish men during a ten-year follow-up', *Am J Epidemiology*, vol 127, pp 28–41 (1988).

20 Patterson, R.E. et al., 'Vitamin supplements and cancer risk: the

epidemiological evidence', *Cancer Causes and Control*, vol 8, pp 786–802 (1997).

21 Wald, N. et al., 'Plasma retinol, beta-carotene and vitamin E levels in relation to future risk of breast cancer', *Brit J Cancer*, vol 49, pp 321–4 (1984).

22 *Int J Cancer*, vol 65, pp 140–44 (1996).

23 Nesaretnam, K. et al., 'Tocotrienols inhibit the growth of human breast cancer cells irrespective of estrogen receptor status', *Lipids*, vol 33(5), pp 461–9 (1998).

24 *Journal of the National Cancer Institute*, vol 90, pp 440–46 (1998).

25 Albanes, D. et al., 'Effects of alpha-tocopherol and beta-carotene supplements on cancer incidence in the Alpha-Tocopherol and Beta-Carotene Cancer Prevention Study', *Am J Clin Nutr*, vol 62 (6 suppl, pp 1427S–1430S) (1995).

26 Baron, I.A. et al., 'Folate intake, alcohol consumption, cigarette smoking and risk of colorectal adenomas', *J Natl Cancer Inst*, vol 90(1), pp 57–62 (1998).

27 Garland, C.F. et al., 'Dietary vitamin D and calcium and the risk of colorectal cancer: a 19-year prospective study in men', *Lancet*, vol 1 (8424), pp 307–9 (1985).

28 Elias, M., 'Vitamin D may help beat cancer', *USA Today* (26/1/89).

29 Saunders, M.P. et al., 'A novel cycle adenosine monophosphate analog induces hypercalcemia via production of 1.25-dihydroxy vitamin D in patients with solid tumours', *J Clin Endocrinol Metab*, vol 82(12), pp 4044–8 (1997).

30 Kidd, P.M., 'Glutathione: systemic protectant against oxidative and free radical damage', *Alt Med Rev*, vol 2(3), pp 155–75 (1997).

31 Donnerstag, B. et al., 'Reduced glutathione and s-acetylgluta-thione as selective apoptosis-inducing agents in cancer therapy', *Cancer Letters*, vol 110, pp 53–70 (1996).

32 Ohlenschlager, G. and Treusch, G., 'Reduced glutathione and anthocyans – redox recycling and redox reycling in biological systems', *Praxis-telegramm*.

33 Garcia-Giralt, E. et al., 'Preliminary study of GSH I-cysteine anthocyane (Reconstat Compositum – TM) in metastatic colorectal carcinoma with relative denutrition', Seventh International Congress on Anti-Cancer Treatment (February 1997).

34 Folkers, K. et al., 'Relevance of the biosynthesis of coenzyme Q10 and of the four bases of DNA as a rationale for the molecular causes of cancer and a therapy', *Biochem Biophys Res Commun*, vol 224(2), pp 358–61 (1996).
Folkers, K. et al., 'Activities of vitamin Q10 in animal models and a serious deficiency in patients with cancer', *Biochem Biophys Res Commun*, vol 234(2), pp 296–9 (1997).

35 Lockwood, K. et al., 'Progress on therapy of breast cancer with vitamin Q10 and the regression of metastases', *Biochem Biophys Res Commun*, vol 212(1), pp 172–7 (1995).

36 Lockwood, K. et al., 'Apparent partial remission of breast cancer in "high risk" patients supplemented with nutritional antioxidants, essential fatty acids and coenzyme Q10', *Mol Aspects Med*, vol 155, pp S231–S240 (1994).

37 Salonen, J.T. et al., 'Risk of cancer in relation to serum concentrations of selenium and vitamins A and E', *BMJ*, vol 290, pp 17–20 (1985).

38 *Am J Clin Nutr*, vol 64, pp 190–96 (1966).

39 *Cancer Epidemiol Biomarkers Prevention*, vol 6(10), pp 769–74 (1977).

40 Yong, L-C et al., 'Intakes of vitamins E, C and A and risk of lung cancer: the NHANES I epidemiologic follow-up study', *Am J Epidemiol*, vol 146(3), pp 231–43 (1997).

41 Shklar, G. et al., 'The effectiveness of a mixture of beta-carotene, alpha-tocopherol and ascorbic acid for cancer prevention', *Nutrition and Cancer*, vol 20(2) (1993).

42 Willet, W.C. et al., 'Prediagnostic serum selenium and risk of cancer', *Lancet*, vol 11, pp 130–34 (1983).

43 Yu, S-Y et al., 'Regional variation of cancer mortality incidence and its relation to selenium levels in China', *Biol Trace Element Res*, vol 7, pp 21–9 (1985).

44 Fleet, J.C. and Mayer, J., 'Dietary selenium repletion may reduce cancer incidence in people at high risk who live in areas with low soil selenium', *Nutrition Reviews*, vol 55(7), pp 277–86 (1997).

45 Rayman, M., 'Dietary selenium: time to act', *BMJ*, vol 314, pp 387–8 (1997).

46 Ip, C. & Lisk, D.J., 'Modulation of phase I and phase II xenobiotic metabolizing enzymes by selenium-enriched garlic', *Nutr Cancer*, vol 28(2), pp 184–8 (1997).

47 Ip, C. & Lisk, D.J., 'Efficacy of cancer prevention by high-selenium garlic is primarily dependent on the action of selenium', *Carcinogenesis*, vol 16(11), pp 2649–52 (1995).

Ip, C. et al., 'Selenium-enriched garlic inhibits the early stage but not the late stage of mammary carcinogenesis', *Carcinogenesis*, vol 17(9), pp 1979–82 (1996).

48 Clark, L.C. et al., 'Effects of selenium supplementation for cancer prevention in patients with carcinoma of the skin', *JAMA*, vol 276, pp 1957–63 (1996).

49 Interview with Dr Gerhard Schrauzer by Dr Richard Passwater in *Optimum Nutrition*, vol 6(1) (1993).

50 Negri, E. et al., 'Intake of selected micronutrients and the risk of breast cancer', *Int J Cancer*, vol 65(2), pp 140–44 (1966).

51 Wargovich, M.J. et al., 'Calcium supplementation decreases rectal epithelial cell proliferation in patients with colorectal adenoma', *Gastroenterology*, vol 103(1), pp 92–7 (1992).

52 Carroll, K. et al., 'Calcium and carcinogenesis of the mammary gland', *Am J Clin Nutr*, vol 54, pp 2068–88 (1991).

53 Whelen, P. et al., 'Zinc, vitamin A and prostatic cancer', *Brit J Urology*, vol 55(5), pp 525–8 (1983).

Habib, F.K. et al., 'Metal-androgen interrelationships in carcinoma and hyperplasia of the human prostrate', *J Endocrinol*, vol 71(1), pp 33–41 (1976).

Romics, I. and Katchalova, L., 'Spectrographic determination of zinc in the tissues of adenoma and carcinoma of the prostate', *Int Urol Nephrol*, vol 15(2), pp 171–6 (1983).

54 Cyong, J.C. et al., *J Ethno Pharmacol*, vol 19, pp 279–83 (1987).

55 Kazuyoshi, M. et al., 'A desmutagenic factor isolated from burdock', *Mutation Research*, vol 129, pp 25–31 (1984).

56 Cerri, R. et al., *Nat Prod*, vol 51, p 257 (1988).

57 Erhard, M. et al., 'Effects of Echinacea, Aconium, Lachesis and Apis extracts and their combinations on phagocytosis of human granulocytes', *Phytother Res*, vol 8, pp 14–17 (1994).

58 Zhang, L. and Tizard, I.R., 'Activation of a mouse macrophage cell line by acemannan: the major carbohydrate fraction from Aloe vera gel', *Immunopharmacology*, vol 35(2), pp 119–28 (1996).

59 Nanba, H., 'MaitakeD-fraction: healing and preventive potential for cancer', *J of Orthomolecular Med*, vol 12(1), pp 43–9 (1997).

60 Wang, S.Y. et al., 'The anti-tumour effect of Ganoderma lucidum is mediated by cytokines released from activated macrophages and T lymphocytes', *Int J Cancer*, vol 70(6), pp 699–705 (1997).

61 Lin, J.M. et al., 'Radical scavenger and antihepatotoxic activity of Ganoderma formosanum, Ganoderma lucidum and Ganoderma neo-japonicum', *J Ethnopharmacol*, vol 47(1), pp 33–41 (1995).

62 Zhao, K. et al., 'Enhancement of immune response in mice by Astragulus membranaceus', *Immunopharmacol*, vol 20, pp 225–33 (1990).

63 You, W. et al., *J Natl Cancer Inst*, vol 81(2), pp 162–4 (1989).

64 Steinmetz et al., *Am J Epid*, vol 139(1), pp 1–15 (1994).

65 Singletary, K. and Smith, M.A., *Traco Labs Inc, Champaign II.*

66 Kamie, H. et al., 'Flavonoid-mediated tumour growth suppression demonstrated by in vivo study', *Cancer Biotherapy and Radiopharmaceuticals*, vol 11(3) (1996).

67 Katiyar, S.K. et al., 'Protective effects of silymarin against photocarcinogenesis in a mouse skin model', *Natl Cancer Inst*, vol 89(8), pp 556–66 (1997).

68 Zi, X. et al., 'Anticarcinogenic effect of a flavonoid antioxidant, silymarin, in human breast cancer cells MDA-MB 468: induction of GI arrest through an increase in cyp concommitant with a decrease in kinase activity of cyclin-dependent kinases and associated cyclins', *Clin Cancer Res*, vol 4(4), pp 1055–64 (1998).

69 Kuttan, R. et al., 'Potential anticancer activity of turmeric (Curcuma longa)', *Cancer Lett*, vol 29, pp 197–202 (1985)
Soudamini, N.K. and Kuttan, R., 'Inhibition of chemical carcinogenesis by curcumin', *J Ethnopharmacol*, vol 27, pp 227–33 (1989).

70 Gerard, G., 'Therapeutique anti-cancreuse et bromelaines', *Agressologie*, vol 3, pp 261–74 (1972).

Part 5

1 Epstein, S., Steinman, D. and LeVert, S., *The Breast Cancer Prevention Programme*, Macmillan, New York (1997).

2 Early Breast Cancer Trials Collaborative Group. 'Systemic treatment of early breast cancer by hormonal, cytotoxic or immune therapy', *The Lancet*, vol 339 (1992).

3 'Studies spark Tamoxifen controversy', *Science News* (26 February 1994).

4 Simone, C.B. 'Use of therapeutic levels of nutrients to augment oncology care', In eds Quillin, P. and Williams, M., *Adjuvant Nutrition in Cancer Treatment*, Academic Press, Tulsa, OK, vol 72 (1992).
Simone, C.B. et al., 'Nutritional and lifestyle modification to augment oncology care: an overview.' *J Orthomolecular Med*, vol 12(4), pp 97–206 (1997).

5 Myers, C.E. et al., 'Adriamycin amelioration of toxicity by alpha-tocopherol', *Cancer Treat Rep*, vol 60, pp 961–2 (1976).
Simone, C.B. et al., op. cit.

6 Folkers, K. and Yamura, Y. (eds), *Biomedical and Clinical Aspects of Coenzyme Q*, Amsterdam; Elsevier/Netherland Biomedical Press, vol 2, pp 333–47 (1980).

7 Nieper, H.A., 'Bromelain in der kontrolle malignen Waschstums', *Krebsgeschehen*, vol 1, pp 9–15 (1976).

8 Muscaritoli, M. et al., 'Oral glutamine in the prevention of chemotherapy-induced gastrointestinal toxicity', *Eur J Cancer*, vol 33(2), pp 319–20 (1997).

9 Ziegler, T.R. et al., 'Clinical and metabolic efficacy of glutamine-supplemented parenteral nutrition after bone marrow transplantation', *Ann Intern Med*, vol 116, pp 821–8 (1992).

10 Austgen, T.R. et al., 'The effects of glutamine-enriched total parenteral nutrition on tumour growth and host tissues', *Ann Surg*, vol 215(2), pp 107–13 (1992).
Souba, W.W., 'Glutamine and cancer', *Ann Surg*, vol 218, pp 715–28 (1993).
Rouse, K. et al., 'Glutamine enhances selectivity of chemotherapy through changes in glutathione metabolism', *JPEN*, vol 17(28S) (1993).
Klimberg, V.S., et al., 'Glutamine facilitates chemotherapy while reducing toxicity', *JPEN*, vol 16(1S), pp 83S–87S (1992).

RECOMMENDED READING

Our Stolen Future, Theo Colborn, Myers and Dumanoski, Little Brown (1996)

The Feminization of Nature, Deborah Cadbury, Hamish Hamilton (1997)

Genetic Nutritioneering, Dr Jeffrey Bland, Keats Publishing (1999)

Healing Foods, Dr Rosy Daniel, HarperCollins (1996)

How to Live Longer and Feel Better, Linus Pauling Ph.D., W.H. Freemand and Co. New York (1986)

Getting Well Again, O. Carl Simonton MD, Stephanie Matthews-Simonton and James L. Creighton, Bantam Books (1978)

Cancer and Its Nutritional Therapies, Dr Richard Passwater, Keats Publishing (1993)

Daylight Robbery, Dr Damien Downing, Arrow Books (1988)

Sharks Don't Get Cancer, Dr William Lane, Avery Publishing Group (1992)

Love, Medicine and Miracles, Dr Bernie Siegel, Harper and Row Publishers (1986)

Food, Nutrition and the Prevention of Cancer: a global perspective, World Cancer Research Fund/American Institute for Cancer Research (1997) – summary available

The Ecologist, vol 28(2), (March/April 1998)

The Optimum Nutrition Bible, Patrick Holford, Piatkus (1997)

USEFUL ADDRESSES

Institute for Optimum Nutrition (ION)
ION offers personal consultations with qualified nutrition consultants and courses including the one-day Optimum Nutrition Workshop, the Homestudy Course and the three-year Nutrition Consultants Diploma Course. They also have a Directory of Nutrition Consultants (£2) to help you find one in your area. For details on courses, consultations and publications, send a stamped addressed envelope to:

ION, Blades Court, Deodar Road, London SW15 2NU.
Tel: 0181 877 9993 or Fax: 0181 877 9980 or visit
www.optimumnutrition.co.uk

Nutrition Consultations
For personal referral by Patrick Holford to a clinical nutritionist in your area please write to **Holford & Associates**, 34 Wadham Road, London SW15 2LR, stating your name, address, telephone number and brief details of your health issue (for overseas requests include your fax or email) or visit *www.patrickholford.com*

Nutritional Supplements are available from a wide variety of companies. Two companies that provide an extensive range, between them covering the speciality supplements referred to in this book are **Solgar**, available in healthfood shops (Tel: 01442 890355 for your nearest stockist) and **Higher Nature** available by mail order (Tel: 01435 882880 for further details). **Rejuvan Forte** is a combination of anthocyans and reduced glutathione. It is available from pharmacies and by mail order – Tel: 01932 889222.

The Nutritional Cancer Therapy Trust

The Trust is a charity which supports cancer patients, using its nutritional therapy. It also aims to research and advise on the use of natural and holistic therapies for the treatment of cancer.

Skyecroft, Wonham Way, Gomshall, Surrey GU5 9NZ.
Tel: 01483 202264 Fax: 01483 203130

Wessex Cancer Help Centre

The Centre offers support, information and a regular newsletter.

8 South Street, Chichester, West Sussex PO19 1EH.
Tel: 01243 778516

Bristol Cancer Help Centre

The Centre offers advice on a wide range of therapies that provide a holistic approach to dealing with cancer. They have a doctor's phone-in, sell information packs and have a two-day stay which includes group sessions, counselling for carers, healing and individual appointments with a doctor, healer, counsellor and dietician. Week-long follow-ups are also on offer.

Grove House, Cornwallis Grove, Clifton, Bristol BS8 4PG.
Tel: 0117 980 9500

Nutri-Link

Nutri-Link is the UK distributor for the cancer protection panel – a sophisticated DNA profile test which can determine whether a person has inherited certain oncogenes, and whether or not they have been activated. The tests are carried out in the USA by Immunosciences Lab Inc. To find the nearest health care practitioner to you who can provide the test, Tel: 01626 205417.

Wholistic Research Company

The company sells a wide range of products including water distillers, computer screen filters, juicers and much more. Tel: 01954 781074.

INDEX

Ever wish you were better informed?

100% HEALTH NEWSLETTER & TAPE

If you want to be in the front line of what's new and exciting in health and nutrition there is no better way than subscribing to **100% Health**, Patrick Holford's newsletter and tape. Considered the hottest voice in alternative healthcare today, Patrick Holford will share with you the very latest discoveries in a way that you can incorporate into your life. More of a journey of discovery than a journal, with each issue of his newsletter and 90 minute CD or audio tape you'll have a new piece of the jigsaw of **100% health**.

FREE-TRIAL NO-RISK SUBSCRIPTION Join NOW and receive a FREE tape and newsletter. Your first issue comes free and, if you decide to continue your subscription, your subscription starts with the second issue. You pay £29 a year and receive 4 audio tapes and 4 newsletters. If you decide the first issue of the **100% Health Newsletter and tape** is not for you you'll receive a full refund within 10 days of notification. Call +44 (0)20 8871 2949 giving your address and credit card details or subscribe by visiting *www.patrickholford.com*.

100% HEALTH SEMINARS

Take the first step to health by enrolling in one of Patrick Holford's seminars and work-shops. These range from evening events to one day workshops on a wide range of sub-jects and four day intensives for doctors and other health care professionals. For a full schedule of events visit *www.patrickholford.com* or call +44 (0)20 8871 2949 for a list of events near you.

100% HEALTH CONSULTATIONS

For personal referral by Patrick Holford to a clinical nutritionist in your area specialising in your area of health concern, please write to **Holford & Associates, 34 Wadham Road, London SW15 2LR**. Enclose your name, address, telephone number and brief details of your health issue. Postal and telephone consultations are available for those overseas. Full details are given on *www.patrickholford.com*.

See what others say about Patrick Holford's work:

"If you want informative, alternative information you can trust, Patrick Holford is the man. His work is completely brilliant." *Hazel Courteney, Sunday Times*

"Patrick Holford is guiding the nutrition revolution. Great work." *Dr Jeffrey Bland, Health-Comm Clinical Research Centre*

"I am dazzled by the breadth of his nutritional knowledge. Patrick Holford has absorbed a tremendous mass of disconnected data and put it together in a simple way that makes immediate sense for the rest of us. Areas of complexity and confusion in nutrition are explained in clear, concise terms, understandable by all." *Dr John Lee MD, author of "What Your Doctor Didn't Tell You About the Menopause"*

"This is do-it-yourself health at its best." *Here's Health magazine*